WEALTH AS PERIL AND OBLIGATION

Sondra Ely Wheeler

WEALTH AS PERIL AND OBLIGATION

The New Testament on Possessions

William B. Eerdmans Publishing Company
Grand Rapids, Michigan

255 Jefferson Ave. S.E., Grand Rapids, Michigan 49503

Printed in the United States of America

00 99 98 97 96 95 7 6 5 4 3 2 1

Library of Congress Cataloging-in-Publication Data

Wheeler, Sondra Ely, 1949-

Wealth as peril and obligation: the New Testament on possessions /Sondra Ely Wheeler.

p. cm.

Includes bibliographical references (p.).

ISBN 0-8028-0733-X (alk. paper)

1. Wealth — Biblical teaching. 2. Ethics in the Bible. 3. Bible.

N.T. — Criticism, interpretation, etc. I. Title.

BS2545.W37W44 1995

241′.69′09015 — dc20 95-9161

CIP

To my parents

Russell Ely and Catherine Hasselman Ely

who taught me what I know about generosity

Contents

Acknowledgments

ONE OF THE GREATEST PLEASURES of finishing a project like this is the opportunity it provides to thank publicly the people who contribute their time, their patience, and their expertise to seeing it done better than could otherwise have been hoped for. Like many books, this one began its life as a doctoral dissertation, in this case written from 1990 to 1992 at Yale University, where I was extraordinarily fortunate in having two fine scholars and teachers as advisors. Gene Outka, Dwight Professor of Christian Ethics at Yale, did his best to keep my prose clear and my conclusions sound, and was unfailingly kind and supportive through the sometimes harrowing journey of those years. Whatever remains turgid or wrongheaded in what follows is certainly not his fault. Richard B. Hays, now Associate Professor of New Testament at Duke University Divinity School, graciously agreed to serve as codirector of the dissertation, and has continued to be available as consultant and critic since then while his own book on New Testament ethics has been in progress. He is also the person who initiated my interest in the problem of method in New Testament ethics back in my first year of seminary, and I have benefited enormously from our ongoing conversation. Both of these men have been much more than advisors to me over the years; I have a lively sense of how much I owe them as teachers, examples, and friends.

I also thank Margaret Farley, Gilbert L. Stark Professor of Christian Ethics at Yale Divinity School. Her comments and questions clarified the scope and improved the execution of the dissertation project, and her encouragement brought me to undertake its revision and publication. My debt to the work of Wayne A. Meeks, Professor of Religious Studies at Yale University, is evident throughout the text (although I am solely responsible for the constructive use to which it is put). In addition, his comments as reader forced me to clarify and strengthen the argument at crucial points. I also acknowledge the assistance of Ken Harrington, a student at Wesley Theological Seminary who served as text editor for the finished manuscript.

Finally, it is a cliche to thank one's spouse for the thousand kinds of support and encouragement that are required from the partner of anyone who undertakes a task like this. In my case, though, the support has been even greater than usual. My husband played a major role in seeing this book written, ranging from caring for the son who was born halfway through the original draft to solving the computer emergencies that threatened to devour its pages without a trace. It is no exaggeration at all to say that I could not have done it without him.

Introduction

IT IS WIDELY AGREED that the New Testament is in some sense authoritative for Christian theology, including Christian ethics. But the enormous range of theological and ethical proposals that have been put forward as "biblically based," and their frank disagreements with each other, force us to become aware of all the questions that lie between the avowal of biblical authority and any substantive theological or ethical proposal. How these questions are answered by a given interpreter will decisively affect how she or he can appropriate the moral witness of the New Testament and what form her or his appeals to the canon as a moral authority can take.

Thus, the wide variety of ethical claims that cite the New Testament as a major or controlling source for Christian ethics is not due only to the complexities of exegesis or hermeneutics, vexing as these may be. In larger part, it is a reflection of different answers to the question, What is it in or about the New Testament that is morally authoritative for the contemporary church?[1] This is a question not only about the use of Scripture but about the basic tasks of Christian ethics and about the appropriate structure for Christian moral discourse.

Insofar as Christian ethics addresses the question, How ought we to live? (and it does this among many other things), what is its overall shape? A number of candidates for a general description exist, including many that command wide acceptance. There is St. Augustine's commendation of a "rightly ordered love," in which a proper love for each created thing

1. This is in turn one aspect of the differing conceptions of, and strategies for, the appropriation of Scripture in theology that David Kelsey has so illuminatingly outlined in his book, *The Uses of Scripture in Recent Theology* (Philadelphia: Fortress Press, 1975).

will direct us to our fulfillment in God. There are Luther's (and Paul's) description of "faith working through love,"[2] and Allen Verhey's effort to discern "the shape of a life worthy of the gospel,"[3] also Pauline. There are H. Richard Niebuhr's "inquiry into the Christian manner of life,"[4] Reinhold Niebuhr's "search for the distinctive contribution of religion to morality,"[5] and Paul Ramsey's formulation of ethical principles to guide moral decision making.

Most of these inquiries can in turn be understood in diverse ways, centering on the goals that are to be served, or on the character and motivation of agents, or on the moral examples and ideals that are to be imitated or pursued, or on the duties that are to be performed as central to the Christian life and its inculcation. Each conception of the task at hand shapes a methodology and a corresponding kind of appeal to Scripture. The thoroughgoing consequentialist searches for a more or less coherent telos against which to measure the morality of acts, and the deontologist looks for laws or expressions of obligation. Appealing to different strands of the text are those who look to Scripture to commend and exemplify desirable qualities of character.[6] Yet other aspects of the canon are appropriated by those who look there for the "revealed reality of God," to whom we respond in our moral lives.[7]

In recent studies, divergent accounts of the central task of Christian ethics, and the markedly different readings of the Bible that have shaped and been shaped by them, have brought issues of method to the fore. The authors of serious attempts to make or criticize proposals about the use of Scripture in Christian ethics frequently follow Gustafson's early lead[8] in

2. *Commentary on the Epistle to the Galatians.*

3. *The Great Reversal* (Grand Rapids: Eerdmans, 1984), p. 2.

4. *The Responsible Self* (San Francisco: Harper and Row, 1978), p. 3.

5. *An Interpretation of Christian Ethics* (New York: Seabury Press, 1979), p. 2.

6. Among recent writers, one thinks of Stanley Hauerwas in *A Community of Character* and *The Peaceable Kingdom;* J. H. Yoder; and Gilbert Meilaender. Recent Roman Catholic work on the virtues also seeks biblical warrants.

7. The term is Gustafson's, in his distinction between moral and theological uses of Scripture in the seminal article "The Place of Scripture in Ethics: A Methodological Study," reprinted in *Theology and Ethics* (Philadelphia: Pilgrim Press, 1974). Such a construal of the role of the Bible in the doing of ethics can be observed in H. R. Niebuhr's *The Responsible Self.*

8. In the 1970 article previously cited, "The Place of Scripture in Ethics," originally in *Interpretation* 24, October 1970.

explicitly outlining various options and in rejecting or endorsing or modifying them for their own work. This has generated a number of useful (though generally incomplete) summaries of the methodological alternatives.[9] Moreover, it has had the salutary effect of creating a level of self-consciousness that eliminates at least the worst faults of a cavalier and inconsistent use of Scripture. In some cases, attention to the complexities of movement from the Bible to ethical assertions has been instrumental in the formulation of thoughtful and sophisticated methodological proposals. These have addressed the ways in which biblical material in general and the New Testament in particular can provide resources for moral formation, reflection, and decision making.

One of my aims in this book is to lend that developing conversation about method greater concreteness and specificity by focusing on a particular question and by closely examining particular texts. Of course, the choice of what particular question and which texts is no accident. The question of the moral status of wealth, and the relation of Christian faith to issues of economic justice and responsibility, seems to me one of the areas in which Christians are most confused, divided, and uneasy. As a contribution to a much-needed discussion of these issues within the church, I here address the following question: How can the New Testament canon form and inform the contemporary moral discernment of the church regarding the holding and use of possessions?

As a starting point, in the first chapter I will offer a brief critical review of the general methodological work six different theorists have done. Based on this review, in the second chapter I will suggest refinements, extensions, and in some cases counterproposals that will in turn form the basis for a constructive methodological proposal. The result will be an outline of how we might go about assessing, ordering, and interpreting the New Testament's moral witness on any particular topic for our own use.

The workability and fruitfulness of this constructive proposal will be tested when I turn to particular texts within the New Testament canon that deal with wealth and possessions. The central four chapters will consist

9. Besides Gustafson's own, see earlier E. L. Long's "The Use of the Bible in Christian Ethics," *Interpretation* 19, April 1965. More recently, Bruce Birch and Larry Rasmussen, *Bible and Ethics in Christian Life* (Minneapolis: Augsburg Publishers, 1976), pp. 45-76, and Verhey, *Great Reversal,* pp. 154-69.

of the exegesis of four passages that I have chosen to represent distinct forms and voices within that canon. I will use primarily the techniques of literary, form, and socio-historical criticism. In addition, the results of these investigations will have to be situated within, and related to, the results of a more comprehensive (and necessarily more cursory) look at the New Testament as a whole. My effort will be to understand the ethical teachings of these passages in relation to the larger theological and parenetic agendas of their various authors. I will indicate how these texts may have functioned within the "moral worlds" of their authors and original hearers. Finally, I will use the results of exegesis, and the methodological guidelines developed for using texts in constructive ethics, to assess the applicability and force of each particular text in our changed social and historical circumstances.

The closing chapters will address the question of how the New Testament witness taken as a whole can and should shape the reflection and judgment of the modern Christian church regarding the moral status of possessions. It will attend to what kinds of theological and ethical significance wealth and property are held to have in the New Testament, what tests and principles it employs for the moral assessment of economic life, and how these may continue to function for us.

The effort to relate the New Testament witness "as a whole" raises all the complex problems of synthesis. My attempt to draw general normative conclusions will necessarily involve extensive discussion of how the diversity of the New Testament canon and even the disagreements between various texts can be recognized and accommodated and how decisions can be reached about what will govern the church's common life.

Regarding the ethics of ownership, I do not intend to establish rules about acceptable levels of income or material comfort, or to propose any single pattern of economic life as the one "authorized" by the New Testament. Neither will I seek to provide material for a formal moral casuistry about wealth. I wish simply to assess and to order what the New Testament can contribute to the ethics of property, and to use those contributions to provide tools and criteria for moral discernment within contemporary Christian communities.

On the larger question of the relation between the Bible and other moral sources, I want to be clear about what I do and do not intend to assert in this book. First, I do not intend to imply that the New Testament in isolation simply determines either the content or the agenda of Christian ethics. It would be nonsense to pretend that we face no new questions or situations, or that the social and historical changes of two millennia have no impact on how we ought to behave. Nor do I suppose that, having come to some conclusions about what the New Testament has to tell us about the ethics of ownership (or any other topic), we will have completed our moral reflection on the subject. It is unimaginable that Christians of any time or place might make concrete decisions about what to do with property without any attention to the economic realities within which their actions would take place; I take for granted that the circumstances that determine the consequences of actions must inform our moral reflection about them. Therefore I assume that various noncanonical sources, including social scientific data about the distribution of wealth and the economic effects of possible actions, are relevant to the process of making specific determinations about practice.

At the same time, I do want to make some positive claims for the appropriateness, indeed the necessity, of beginning our moral discernment on this or any topic with disciplined attention to the actual content of the New Testament. For I also assume that the New Testament remains the central and definitive source for the theological affirmations that constitute the church and that its role is therefore crucial in the formation of any distinctively Christian ethics. There are contemporary issues (in bioethics, or the use of technology, or for that matter in macroeconomics) that the New Testament can address only in the most general and oblique fashion. Nonetheless, in its account of God's action in Jesus Christ and in its call for conduct that conforms to that action, it establishes the horizons of Christian moral life. The criteria it provides can determine much of what enters into consideration as possible moral alternatives from a Christian standpoint, and can rule out otherwise defensible norms for conduct. Our reading of it will shape what count as morally relevant considerations even in those many circumstances that are, in the nature of the case, never directly addressed.

It is evident that the New Testament cannot and will not answer all the moral questions that we might put to it. Besides the historical distance already alluded to, we deal with Scripture's resolute insistence on the indissolubility of theology and ethics. To the extent that we as moderns live in a religiously pluralistic world and frame our questions in neutral terms of universal practical reason or constructive social policy, the New Testament will not respond with similar neutrality. It may be that the greatest service its canon can do us as Christian ethicists is to force us to recognize when our questions, including our questions about the moral status of wealth and possessions, are inadequate. It may lead us to rethink and reformulate them, bringing into greater focus those things the New Testament affirms as the sum and point of moral life: the love of God and neighbor.

CHAPTER 1

Critical Review of Methodological Proposals

Common Ground

IT IS BOTH NATURAL AND NECESSARY to begin this exploration of how we might use the New Testament to do constructive contemporary ethics with a review of the conversation about method to date. Such a review not only gives a valuable context for the present discussion but makes clear both how much I am in debt to the various contributors to that conversation and where and why I differ from them. Before reviewing the details of earlier efforts to deal with the problem of method, I will summarize the insights they have in common as a foundation for the work that follows.

First, all of them agree that in order to claim an identity as Christian ethics, any proposal must be able to display *some* connection to the New Testament as the single witness to the historical events and confessional claims that constitute the Christian church. (How and to what degree that witness controls the content of those proposals is, of course, a major point at issue.)

All have drawn attention to the great diversity of kinds of material in the New Testament, and to the necessity of reading, for example, Matthew's record of the teaching of Jesus somewhat differently from the narratives of Acts or the theological discourses of Paul. The basic requirement of sound exegesis that passages be read with some sensitivity to their literary and historical context has been observed to apply to their use for ethics as well — an obvious enough point, but one often ignored in practice.

It is also generally accepted that Christian ethics properly refers to a number of different subjects and inquiries and that the diversity of biblical materials might be brought to bear on these different questions in different ways. Tasks that range from explicating the meaning of language about good and evil to considering the end of human life to evaluating particular moral claims call not for one fixed method appealing to one form within the text, but for a variety of methods that can appropriate the whole range of New Testament discourse. The necessity of a balanced treatment that gives proper weight to the entire canonical witness has been given varying degrees of emphasis by different writers, but is acknowledged in principle by all.

Finally, common to most of these proposals is an effort to take account of the eschatological thrust of much of the New Testament in a manner that does not vitiate the force of the ethical enterprise, but rather strengthens and enriches it.

Framing the Question: The Contribution of James Gustafson

Few short articles have had more influence than James Gustafson's aforementioned essay, "The Place of Scripture in Ethics." Gustafson contributed a badly needed clarity to the discussion by distinguishing between a variety of what he called moral (as opposed to theological) uses of Scripture. He describes three patterns of appeal to the canon as "revealed morality," and adds a fourth that he calls an appeal to "revealed reality."

First under the heading of appeals to the canon as "revealed morality," he considers appeals to the Bible as a source of moral laws. This pattern he finds inadequate due to ambiguities both in content and in application of the law. A second kind of appeal, to moral goals and ideals of character, he sees as problematic because of the complications introduced by eschatology. What degree of approximation to biblical ideals of character and conduct is to be looked for under present conditions? Gustafson's third category of "revealed morality" is the use of Scripture to provide models or analogies by which to judge moral acts. Acts are to be judged by comparison with those seen as in or out of accord with God's will in the Bible. Here Gustafson voices the suspicion that prior moral judgments will determine which biblical events are used as analogies for contemporary situations.

Preferable to all of these Gustafson finds what he calls the "great variety" model of biblical ethics. This use of the Bible, which Gustafson describes as "looser" than the other three, emphasizes the variety of forms of moral discourse in Scripture and their resistance to being reduced to a single theme. Their rootedness in particular historical contexts leads him to conclude that moral judgments can only be made "in light of" appeals to this material as well as to other sources and principles: "Scripture is one of the informing sources for moral judgments, but it is not sufficient of itself to make any particular judgment authoritative."[1]

This judgment is in line with Gustafson's own preference for seeing Scripture not as a revealed morality to which Christians must adhere, but rather as the primary source for the "revealed reality" of God to which Christians must respond in their moral lives.[2] Scripture is the source of data for answering questions about God's character or nature and about the history of his actions toward and on behalf of his people. These in turn provide the basis for judgments about what God is doing in the contemporary world and about "what God is enabling and requiring men *[sic]* to do under the natural, historical and social conditions in which they live."[3] Gustafson acknowledges that such an appeal requires generalizations about what themes and patterns are central and most significant and decisions about what biblical theological concepts will be used to provide an evaluative description of historical events. Such a process is described by Gustafson as a dialectic between the text and moral judgments and intuitions based upon other sources. The appeal to all of these would be not on the basis of their "authority" but as "corroboration of judgments informed by a variety of appeals."[4]

Gustafson is quick to recognize the enormous problem such a stance creates: "It would be very easy to make a judgment on the basis of feelings or prevailing cultural values and then find some support for it in the variety of Scripture's texts."[5] He acknowledges that his method leaves wide open the questions of control and of the decisiveness of the moral witness of

1. Gustafson, "Place of Scripture," p. 34.

2. Gustafson identifies his position with a larger shift in twentieth-century theological ethics exemplified by people like H. Richard Niebuhr, and discusses it at greater length in his introduction to Niebuhr's book, *The Responsible Self.*

3. Gustafson, "Place of Scripture," p. 141.

4. Ibid., p. 140.

5. Ibid., p. 134.

Scripture. He insists, however, that "the maintenance of any objective authority for the moral witness of Scripture is difficult if one recognizes the variety of norms and values present there and also the historical character of the occasions in which these emerged."[6] Gustafson's position is that there is no alternative to the relativizing effect of his method, because the nature of the New Testament material precludes any other appropriation for ethics. We must resort to efforts at generalization guided by philosophical and theological decisions that may only be "informed" by the Bible.

Such a conclusion seems unwarranted, since it appears to assume that the "variety of norms and values" are without any intelligible relation to one another or to the range of tasks belonging to ethics as an enterprise. It implies that the prescriptive materials directed to their concrete historical situations bear no discernible relation to the larger "priorities of biblical morality"[7] that Gustafson wishes to abstract from the canon as a whole. These assumptions are belied by hints in his own discussions, as he suggests that there might be a place in his model for appeals to moral rules, ideals, and analogies that would not fall into the error of what he calls "proof-texting."

He provides one such hint in a brief article entitled "The Relation of the Gospels to the Moral Life."[8] Here Gustafson explores the way in which Jesus Christ is presented in the Gospels as a model or paradigm for the Christian life. In one of his very rare treatments of a particular New Testament text, Gustafson discusses the role of the story of the foot-washing incident in John 13 in modeling and motivating the dispositions of love and humility within the church. He explicitly says that both the narrative depiction of Jesus' actions and the direct admonitions it contains ("I have given you an example, that you also should do as I have done") have their part in forming moral character.

Here apparently is a way in which specific biblical texts including directives can function morally within the community without distortion. This would hardly be the case if no relationship could be discerned between them and the more general moral appeals Gustafson regards as appropriate.

6. Ibid.

7. Ibid., p. 135.

8. Originally published in *Jesus and Man's Hope,* ed. D. G. Miller and D. Y. Hadidian (Pittsburgh: Pittsburgh Theological Seminary, 1971).

Despite this suggestion, however, one must look elsewhere for a more illuminating treatment of what those relations might be and what they imply for the use of these texts for Christian ethics. Neither in this essay nor elsewhere does Gustafson deal in any extended way with particular passages or their moral implications.

Authority and Levels of Discourse: Birch and Rasmussen

The proposal put forward by Birch and Rasmussen[9] organizes its constructive comments according to the pair of categories "the ethics of being" and "the ethics of doing." The first of these involves all those aspects of the moral life that we think of as being intrinsic to the moral agent, such things as motives, dispositions, and intentions. The second category relates to the concrete acts and decisions of the agent. It concerns judgments of moral obligation aimed at answering the question, What ought I to do? Central to Birch and Rasmussen's proposal are the claims that it is the former category of character formation that is most important and that this is the area in which the Bible ought to have the most decisive impact.

They emphasize the centrality of the individual's basic objects of love and loyalty to the formation of identity, including moral identity. Their account of the place of the Bible in the formation of Christian identity is rich and complex, beginning with its commendation of God and Christ as the ultimate object of trust and source of value. The New Testament establishes the horizons of Christian life as a life of response to the God who is made known in Jesus. Birch and Rasmussen's description of the operation of the Bible in the moral formation of Christians, its setting in the church, and its way of providing the framework within which all explicitly ethical discourse will be conducted is nuanced and very provocative. It is given short shrift here because the account it deserves would be lengthy, and much of its content will be represented in later constructive discussion. Instead I will focus on other aspects of their proposal that are less persuasive (and also less central to their work), because these serve to

9. Birch and Rasmussen, *Bible and Ethics,* 1976 ed. A later edition of this work (1989) is designed for use as an introductory level textbook, and treats specific issues of method in less detail. For this reason, all references are to the 1976 edition.

raise the problems still in need of attention. These aspects concern the role of the Bible in the area of ethics dealing with concrete acts and judgments of particular cases.

Birch and Rasmussen divide the elements of moral decision making into three elements: analysis of the issue and its context, agreement as to the method of reaching a decision, and the elaboration and application of norms. They see the role and decisiveness of the Bible's influence as varying across these elements, playing the least significant role in the analytic phase, where indeed the text may have no point of direct contact. They observe that no single method of moving from general principle to specific application is presented in the Bible, and conclude that a variety of methods of practical moral reasoning may be given biblical support. The Bible's contribution at the level of evaluative standards is greater, although here it may still be either direct or quite indirect, specific (as in an injunction or prohibition) or very general (as in the provision of an ideal of service to persons).

Aside from the provision of norms or standards of judgment peculiar to itself, Birch and Rasmussen assert that the biblical witness may serve to "rank, illumine or transform"[10] norms provided by other sources. Alternatively, it may rule out norms that might otherwise recommend themselves, declaring them out of bounds for Christian ethics. Here the problem of the relation of Scripture to other sources of moral insight is raised. How is the authority of the New Testament in particular seen to operate, especially in the criticism or rejection of norms and rules provided by nonbiblical sources? Conversely, how, if at all, are the insights and moral claims offered by the secular disciplines of philosophy or natural and social science to be allowed to influence, correct, or supersede those of the canon, particularly in the realm of concrete moral rules and judgments? The answers to these questions offered in this proposal seem frustratingly evasive.

On the one hand, Birch and Rasmussen repeatedly affirm that the Bible is and must be normative for the Christian life; so much is inherent in calling it "Scripture." They define "authoritative" as "a source of decisive influence,"[11] and cite James Barr's discussion of authority as a "relational or hierarchical concept" that "tries to order or grade the sources that may

10. Birch and Rasmussen, *Bible and Ethics,* p. 114.
11. Ibid., p. 144.

influence us."[12] On the other hand, they are also careful to assert that the Bible is not the only source of moral authority and that its authority is not absolute. The Bible's authority is "necessary" and "inescapable" and "must be taken into account," but it is "not self-sufficient," and "it is not a sufficiently broad base for making ethical judgments in the modern church."[13] The appropriate relation between biblical and nonbiblical sources, they repeatedly affirm, is "dialogic," and the Bible supplies "not the last word but the necessary framework" in moral deliberation.[14] Insofar as this is a claim about the relevance, indeed the necessity, of nonbiblical sources of information and insight in making moral decisions, it is noncontroversial. However, to the extent that the denial of the status of absolute moral authority to the Bible entails the assertion that its specific moral injunctions may be superseded (as is implied in the remarks on slavery and the treatment of women made early in the book)[15] this assertion requires greater specification than it is given here. As it stands, all sorts of questions are begged.

At what level(s) of ethical discourse is the Bible open to challenge and correction by other sources of insight and authority? What kinds of empirical data and what kinds of argument are to be considered sufficient grounds for such judgments? How can these texts serve to criticize, limit, and judge the standards proposed by other cultural voices and at the same time be subject to correction by them? The point is not that any view that fails to take the Bible as absolutely determinative at every level of discourse is granting it insufficient weight. It is rather that their failure to specify *how* the Bible exercises the authority it *is* granted means that this proposal does not satisfactorily address the questions its authors have set themselves.

Nonetheless, they offer certain insights that give direction to the effort to answer those questions still unresolved. The first and most important of these is the reminder that the Bible's authority is derived from its witness to the will of God, which alone is absolute. If we presume that that will is self-consistent, we must be wary of completely identifying the will of God with the particular injunctions of particular texts, at least insofar as these can be seen to vary within the canon itself. Related to this

12. Ibid., p. 145.
13. Ibid., p. 150.
14. Ibid., p. 158.
15. Ibid., p. 46.

is the idea that "biblical authority operates differently depending on the nature [and the unanimity] of the biblical sources that speak to a given issue."[16] Taken together, these raise the possibility that the effort to make sense of the breadth and diversity of the canon itself might illuminate and control the task of relating biblical and nonbiblical resources; clues may be provided as to which texts operate as governing principles or intentions and which represent their instantiation in a particular setting and circumstance. This possibility in turn relates to a final point of Birch and Rasmussen's argument, that the use of biblical material in the particular arena of decision making requires special attention to the form and context of specific texts if it is to avoid distorting the very text it seeks to honor.

"Licensing and Limiting Moral Appeals": Allen Verhey's Proposal

All of these features — attention to the diversity and tensions within the New Testament canon, the appeal to a variety of kinds and degrees of moral authority for biblical texts, and sensitivity to the interpretive cues of form and context — are characteristic of the next writer whose methodology I will consider, Allen Verhey. Verhey organizes both his descriptive and his constructive remarks around a series of four questions that he identifies as marking the points of divergence of the various methods. Accordingly, I will consider his own proposal in sections corresponding to these same questions.

1. In his discussion of What is the nature of the New Testament text? Verhey tries to steer a middle course between the complete identification of the human word and the divine Word of Scripture and their complete division. This involves recognizing both the human authorship and historical situation of the various texts and the affirmation that what we read in the canon is what the church claims as the Word of God. As Verhey mildly observes, "the conjunction of the human and the divine has always been difficult to be precise about,"[17] and he recognizes that thus far we have not sufficient specificity to warrant (or to rule out) any particular moves from Scripture to moral claim. He offers an example of

16. Ibid., p. 153.
17. *Great Reversal,* p. 170.

the errors he wishes to avoid in the application of the *Haustafeln* texts, disclaiming both their direct use as normative for today and complete disregard of them as regressive and nonnormative.[18] Unfortunately, it is a little difficult to pin down what he wants to do instead.

Verhey's attempt to discern an overarching intention behind texts such as would permit us to "appropriate and apply them in ways and words bound to our own time rather than the first century"[19] involves many risks. Apart from the warnings of literary criticism that authorial intention is simply not available in the texts where we search for it, it is often very difficult in practice to separate a practical rule from the intention that governs it. The example of Matthew's text on divorce that Verhey chooses is a case in point.

Verhey says Matthew's intention is to apply the "disposition toward marriage found in the tradition of Jesus' words" to his own community.[20] This is perfectly plausible. But what is "the disposition toward marriage" that Matthew is trying to apply if it is not that it be regarded as indissoluble? To translate the Gospel's characterization of divorce and remarriage as adulterous into some more general norm, such that it might be expressed or maintained by a different rule, runs the risk of undermining both the force of Jesus' words and the meaning of Matthew's interpretive insertion. Verhey asserts that Matthew's saying about divorce is "neither to be repeated as a moral rule governing judgments about divorce today nor is it to be disowned."[21] Verhey never says precisely what is the alternative that is "faithful and creative," the one that "shares [Matthew's] intention but [applies] it in ways and words bound to our own time."

2. Verhey writes with clarity and deftness about the kinds of questions that are (and are not) appropriate to Scripture. His remarks on the futility of looking to the New Testament for an autonomous ethic suited to governing moral discourse in a pluralistic society[22] are well taken. So are those about the inappropriateness of looking there for an ethical treatise or a comprehensive moral code. But Verhey goes on from these observations, and from a

18. Ibid., p. 172.
19. Ibid., p. 173.
20. Ibid.
21. Ibid.
22. Ibid., pp. 174-76.

principle of respect for the human capacity to give and hear reasons for moral rules, to treat as illegitimate all appeals to the text at the level of moral rule.

> To inquire of Scripture at the "moral-rule" level is to treat it as something it is not and did not intend to be, a moral code. The New Testament must continue to bear on our concrete decisions, not directly, but rather in ways mediated by its responses to inquiries concerning our moral identity, our fundamental loyalty and perspective, and the dispositions and intentions that inhere in that identity. The conclusions, candidly put, are that movements in argument from Scripture to moral claims . . . are authorized at the post-ethical and ethical-principle levels of moral discourse, and are not authorized at the moral-rule level.[23]

Few would argue with Verhey's contention that "the New Testament does not come to us as a timeless moral code dropped from Heaven,"[24] but it is not clear that any and all appeals to the specific commands and prohibitions of the text constitute treating it as such. Nor does this radical account of the difference of normative weight to be ascribed to Scripture at different levels of discourse give any attention to the questions it raises. What does it mean, for example, to ground one's moral reasoning on a morally binding biblical principle of love of neighbor if one gives *no* weight to the Bible's own account of what that neighbor-love concretely entails? Paul is able to say that "love is the fulfilling of the law" because "love does no wrong to a neighbor" (Rom. 13:10), but Paul is quite clear that the content of what love will avoid is specified by the prohibitions of the Decalogue (Rom. 13:8).

While it is evident that the point and purpose of any particular injunction is to be sought in the intention it embodies and the goals it serves, it also seems clear that the *meaning* of any ethical ideal or principle, the substantive content that makes truthfulness or justice or love more than a word, is provided by the concrete demands that give flesh to those principles. It is not that such meaning is exhausted by the sum of its related rules or instances, or even that every rule must be taken as inhering in the principle in every time, place, and situation. But there is a great deal of difference between distinguishing the kind and degree of authority given to concrete rules and underlying principles and failing to grant the specific

23. Ibid., p. 177.
24. Ibid.

moral injunctions of Scripture any authority at all. The latter runs the risk of preserving the ethical principles and ideals Verhey wishes to appeal to as names only, with their content entirely supplied by culturally prevalent norms and definitions.

What is unfortunate in Verhey's proposal is not his refusal to be completely bound by the moral rules in the New Testament, but the appearance that he does not even wish to be seriously challenged or instructed by them.[25]

3. Verhey claims the central message of the New Testament is the affirmation that God, in raising Christ from death, has acted to transform and sanctify creation and to bring it under his reign. Coherence with this claim, at once eschatological and protological, is a testing point for any use of Scripture in moral argument.

4. As one would expect from the foregoing, Verhey's position regarding the relevance of other sources of moral insight varies according to the mode and level of ethical discourse being addressed. At the level of moral rules and the everyday inquiries of What should we do? in the fulfillment of our responsibilities as members of families, professions, human groups, and institutions, the moral content is largely supplied by the behavioral norms belonging to those roles and institutions. At the ethical-principle level, the contribution of secular scientific and philosophical wisdom is still considerable, but now the identity-shaping authority of Scripture comes into play as a source of critical standards that may criticize, transform, or reject the principles offered by other sources. Particular roles, projects, or philosophical and ideological systems may be affirmed and supported as consonant with God's reign over and purposes for the world. However, it is much clearer in Verhey than in other writers we have considered that in this moral dialogue, Scripture has the last and determinative word. At the post-ethical level of discourse, that characterized by the question, Why be moral? the input of Scripture is decisive; Verhey renders its answer bluntly as "because God is God."

Despite the objections raised above, Verhey's work has a great deal

25. From personal correspondence with the author, I understand that this, at least, is not his intention: "I acknowledge the authority of those rules in Scripture. [But] I do not authorize moving directly from a rule in Scripture to a rule today. . . . [T]hat will demand a discerning judgment." If this is taken to mean only that the existence of a rule in the New Testament does not end the discussion of its contemporary applicability, we may have no real quarrel.

to offer us. It gives detailed attention to the variety of decisions or assumptions that are implicit in any appeal to Scripture as moral authority; it offers a clear and specific account of what authorizes such appeals; and in its beginning with the crucial question of what we look to when we look to Scripture, it points up the importance of the basic theological convictions and commitments that pervasively shape both our reading of Scripture and our attempts to honor its authority. It will help to set the agenda in the constructive work that follows.

"The Shaping Story": Scripture and Ethics in the Work of Hauerwas

I turn now to the work of Stanley Hauerwas, primarily as represented in the collection *A Community of Character*[26] and the more recent "primer," *The Peaceable Kingdom.*[27] Central to Hauerwas's construal of the moral authority of Scripture is an ecclesiological claim: the church is constituted by its adherence to the story of the life, death, and resurrection of Jesus Christ. He argues that the Bible grounds an ethic of virtue by providing a foundation for, and narrative display of, those qualities and dispositions that are necessary both to retelling the story and to living in accord with it. Christian virtues are at the same time those characteristics that are made possible by belief in the story and those "which must be formed in the community if it is to make the narratives of Scripture central to its life."[28] It is axiomatic for Hauerwas that the locus of moral discernment is to be the community formed by the use of Scripture in its devotion, its liturgy, and its governance. The necessary task of interpretation, of "building a bridge between the apostolic writings and the present,"[29] must be done by the Christian community as it confronts concrete moral issues.

Hauerwas never makes explicit claims about the relation between canonical and noncanonical sources of moral authority or insight, but something may be inferred from this account of communal decision

26. (Notre Dame: Notre Dame University Press, 1981).
27. (Notre Dame: Notre Dame University Press, 1983).
28. *Community of Character,* p. 68.
29. Ibid., p. 55. This is Hauerwas's quotation of J. H. Yoder's "Radical Reformation Ethics," *Journal of Ecumenical Studies,* Fall 1978.

making.[30] Other moral sources are not ruled out in advance, insofar as they may be expected to inform the judgments of members of the community. On the other hand, the ecclesial setting for moral discernment suggests that primary authority within the community will be granted to the story that gathers and orders that community, whose source is the biblical canon as a whole and the New Testament in particular. And in his own normative ethics, that story is seen to contribute what seem to function as specific and binding prohibitions (most commonly, the rule against the use of force), which presumably exercise control over what may count as reasons or justifications for conduct. The "wisdom of the world" *as such* has no place, and conversely, neither the overarching moral vision of the Christian community nor the particular decisions it reaches are expected to be shared by those who do not share its commitment to the story.

A number of problems arise in Hauerwas's depiction of the moral functioning of Scripture, both in its theoretical aspects of the assumptions it requires about Scripture and in the actual use Hauerwas himself makes of it. The most obvious challenge to his position is that it takes inadequate account of the actual diversity of Scripture. This is not chiefly an objection to his handling of all its various kinds of literature under the heading of narrative; Hauerwas is right to recognize that even Leviticus is placed in a narrative setting, and addressed to a particular audience whose history gives force to the law. Rather it questions his assumption that all of the distinctive and sometimes contradictory stories that form the canon can be made to cohere in a single, morally formative whole. Even if they can, it is not at all clear that Hauerwas has done this in his own use of the text.

Hauerwas insists, rightly I think, that his mode of morally appropriating the Bible requires attention to the whole of the narrative, in all of its historical particularity. He contends that liberal Protestant ethical accounts are defective because "they require little reference to who Jesus was or what he did for their meaning or intelligibility."[31] Yet one cannot help but notice that Hauerwas's own appeals to the concrete words and deeds of Jesus are quite few, and focus almost exclusively on the conflict

30. For a brief discussion of Hauerwas's understanding of the relation between Christian ethics and "native moral insight" see Gene Outka's "Character, Virtue and Narrative," *Religious Studies Review* 6/2, April 1980.

31. *Community of Character,* p. 40.

with the Jewish and Roman authorities that led to his crucifixion. The only direct normative claim of the story on us that Hauerwas addresses is the prohibition of violence.

This is to be our witness to the Lordship of God over history, that which enables the church to embody "the new possibilities of human relationships" made possible by the life, death, and resurrection of Jesus.[32] How compelling a vision this can be is clear to anyone who has read Hauerwas's work. Nor does it lack biblical support; it is, many would argue, a quite defensible reading of the Gospel of Mark. However, even Hauerwas is forced to admit that "we have not one story, but four."[33] Part of the "historical particularity" of the Christian story is that it is many stories, written in different times by people with different ideas. His own reading does not reflect the comprehensive and balanced attention to the whole New Testament canon that the proposal calls for and leads one to expect.

Perhaps most importantly for the purposes of this essay, Hauerwas's reading reveals the interposition between story and ethic of some independently formed judgments about what aspects of the story are crucial (for Hauerwas, nonviolence, trust, acceptance of ambiguity and tragedy) and what are peripheral (notably for this effort, no attention is given to the implications of Jesus' teaching or example regarding wealth). The point is not that such judgments should not be made, but rather that they must be acknowledged and defended for what they are. Hauerwas neglects the degree to which the act of interpretation is a dialectic between the community forming and being formed by the story, and glosses over the difficulties of a community being formed by a body of texts that is itself so multitextured and various. The diversity of the New Testament canon makes interpretive decisions about its central themes necessary; they must be made candidly and with care, and continually tested against the stubborn particularities of the whole canon. Otherwise those decisions will be doing most of the work behind the scenes.

32. *Peaceable Kingdom,* p. 34.
33. *Community of Character,* p. 52.

Thomas Ogletree: A Phenomenological Approach

Ogletree brings to the reading of Scripture the insights of phenomenology and an understanding of interpretation that views it as an act of productive imagination, the product of a dialogue between reader and text. He assumes that the meaning of a text cannot be reduced to the intentions and understandings of its original writers and readers, but that "there is a surplus of meaning beyond what is explicitly uttered,"[34] which arises from the concrete subject matter that it addresses. To understand a text is to find the "shared understanding of the subject matter which provides the common ground between the text and our own inquiries."[35] Therefore, to use the Bible in contemporary ethics, we must formulate the questions to which the text offers itself as answer in ways that are meaningful to us in our vastly different historical setting. This requires attention both to our existing assumptions and frameworks for moral thought and to the structures and assumptions operating in the biblical texts.

Accordingly, Ogletree begins by outlining four different patterns, which he calls "preunderstandings of moral life": he summarizes and points up strengths and weaknesses of teleological, deontological, and virtue theories of morality, and presents a fourth option he identifies as "historical contextualism." This last focuses on the temporal dimensions of human experience as they are implicit in all of these modes of moral thought and on the historical situatedness and dependence of all moral frameworks and concepts. It emphasizes their relativity and final inadequacy, and highlights the larger, pervasive question of the meaning of human existence as it underlies all more particular inquiries.

He then uses these theoretical frames to guide the description and interpretation of materials from different strands of the biblical moral tradition, specifically the law and the prophets, the synoptic Gospels, and Paul. A final chapter suggests themes and perspectives that the author deems useful in our search for common understandings to guide our appropriation of these materials. Here we find treatments of the eschatological thrust of New Testament writings, observations about the normative pressure toward equality in social institutions exerted by Paul's ethic

34. Thomas Ogletree, *The Use of the Bible in Christian Ethics* (Philadelphia: Fortress Press, 1983), p. 2.

35. Ibid., p. 3.

of community, and analyses of the themes of law and promise as they occur throughout the canon.

Although Ogletree disclaims the intention of offering a methodological study, at least the outline of a method is implicit in his constructive statement, and we may focus our attention there. Regarding his preference for the mode he calls "historical contextualism," it is not clear in this presentation at least that this represents a genuine fourth option to consequentialist, deontological, and perfectionist moral theories. It seems rather a second-order reflection on the structures that shape human moral experience and on the status of human moral judgments than a proposal for how moral judgments might be made and justified. More centrally, the dangers Ogletree points to in his discussion of contextualist moral theories[36] (the possibility of a debilitating relativism, the lack of any clear criteria for the constructive appropriation of moral traditions, and the heavy reliance on the moral intuitions of interpreters) all seem to contribute to a major problem of indeterminacy and lack of control. Ogletree wants the process of biblical interpretation he outlines to enable us to "say the same thing differently,"[37] but it is not at all clear how we might test our formulations for whatever "sameness" is desired, or even what might count as evidence.

At the same time, the study has a number of virtues, and makes some salient points about the problem of hermeneutics that are well taken. First and most obvious, its engagement with the texts themselves is serious and sustained, despite having the tour de force quality common to all such summary treatments of the biblical canon. Its use of modern ethical language and categories of thought to organize that treatment is generally illuminating, though issue might be taken with the understanding of various individual texts. Second, by acknowledging and bringing to the fore the fact that the New Testament poses itself as answer to a particular set of questions that are not initially the same as our own, Ogletree prepares the way for a self-conscious and careful act of interpretation. Thus we are less likely to distort the text by forcing it to address what it does not, and less likely to baptize our own moral conclusions as "biblical" when in fact they are not and cannot be.

Finally, Ogletree is extremely helpful in the treatment he gives to the

36. Ibid., pp. 36-37.
37. Ibid., p. 3.

eschatological framework that undergirds so much of the moral discourse of the New Testament.[38] The expectation evident there of Christ's imminent return has often been treated as a "condition contrary to fact" that limits the relevance and vitiates the force of biblical moral norms. More positively, Ogletree understands the eschatological thrust as the biblical answer to the question he poses as "the meaning of being." It is that which conditions the ultimate point and significance of moral life. In the final section, he asserts that the modern church does not need to return to a belief that Christ's return must be imminent in time to establish a point of contact with the eschatologically focused discourse of the New Testament. When and how the parousia is to come about is a question that may be bracketed as secondary. Instead, he suggests that to appropriate the New Testament's eschatological ethic, "the church needs some degree of alienation from the institutional arrangements of the larger society, and [to be] a community which is engaged in developing qualitatively distinct alternatives to those arrangements."[39] More briefly, one might say it needs to be the church. With this provocative suggestion of the necessity of an active community setting for the moral appropriation of Scripture, I turn to a constructive method.

38. Ibid., pp. 177-92.
39. Ibid., p. 182.

CHAPTER 2

A Constructive Proposal

The Moral Authority of Scripture

IF OUR TASK IS TO USE the New Testament in contemporary Christian ethics without distorting it, it is necessary to begin by characterizing the New Testament canon in general. This will tell us something about the role it is suited to play in constructive ethics. Inevitably, encapsulated in any such characterization is something of the interpreter's own basic reading of the texts. We have seen how pervasively any commentator's basic account of What is the New Testament? shapes her understanding and ethical appropriation of Scripture; therefore, it is essential to be candid from the outset about the standpoint from which one begins, and to acknowledge that this point of view is partly taken from and partly *brought to* the reading of Scripture. Here, then, are the working assumptions that inform my own reading, together with what I take to be their implications for the moral use of the New Testament.

Obviously, the New Testament is not an ethical treatise. Indeed, it is not a treatise of any sort, and for the most part it is not about ethics as we generally use the term at all. From one point of view, it is a collection of narratives and letters that tell a story: the story of a man, of the claims that he made and that were made about him, and of what happened to the people who believed those claims and followed him. From another viewpoint, the New Testament is an "in-house" document, part of the internal conversation of the early Christian community as it sought to articulate and pass on a set of beliefs and the way of life that it took to follow from them.

If the church has other than an antiquarian interest in the New

Testament, it is because the church has identified itself with the group of those who believe what is said there about Jesus of Nazareth and because of the nature of those claims. For they are not merely historical reports about which it is possible to be neutral; taken as a whole, they make the astonishing assertion that God has acted in the person and the resurrection of Jesus to enter and redeem and reclaim creation as God's own. They further invite those who accept them into a quite particular relationship with this dead and risen Messiah, that of disciples to a master. Those who believe the claims must accept the relationship; there is no calling Christ Savior without calling him Lord.

But this is not chiefly to be understood as mere obedience, the simple conformity of one's behavior to a set of commands. It is rather that the believer has been brought from death to life, and the appropriate response to this gift and its giver is to offer herself, what she is and does, in return. So fundamental and life shaping is this belonging to God in Christ that "ethics" seems altogether too pale and abstract a term for its impact on how a life is lived. But at least it is clear how the New Testament, if owned as the story both of the world and of oneself, would have everything to do with shaping both reality and identity, and thus with moral life in both character formation and decision making.

The primary importance of this sketch for our larger task lies in the perspective it introduces. It reminds us that to begin the inquiry into the relation between the Bible and Christian ethics with arguments over the applicability of particular rules, or even over the content of particular principles, foreshortens the discussion. It also suggests that while the explicitly ethical material in the New Testament is never dispensable, it is tertiary. It is a response at two removes from the central concerns of the canon, which are concerns about what God has done in Christ and about the relationship God invites human beings to enter as their assent to this gracious act. It is at this level, the construal of reality from which claims of value are derived, that the New Testament can and must speak to the church with unique and definitive authority.

But this account of the place of ethics in the New Testament must not be taken to permit a convenient divorce between God's action and human response. The explicit ideals and norms of Scripture take their force derivatively from their connection with the basic truth claims of this story — but force they do take. Just as the recommended behavior can have no specifically Christian significance apart from being the fruit of a relationship with Christ as Lord, such a relationship can have no substance apart from its instantiation in concrete acts of obedience.

The contention here is that the moral authority of the New Testament for the Christian church arises from the link between its moral teachings and its more basic claims about God's intention to redeem the world through Christ. It is only those who assent to those claims, at least to some central core of them concerning the revelatory power and salvific significance of the life, death, and resurrection of Jesus Christ, who look to these texts for moral guidance. This remains the case even when they are disturbed or offended by what they find there. The church would not protest and wrestle with the elements of sexism or anti-Semitism or complacency toward social evils that it finds in the New Testament if it were not for its recognition that it owes some kind of allegiance to this canon; its moral norms and assumptions matter, whether for good or ill.

But the point here is that Christian allegiance to these texts is not in the first instance as sources of ethical rules or moral advice, but rather as accounts of God's action in Jesus Christ. These are the crucial claims to which believers owe some loyalty, and whose moral consequences have in turn some claim upon them. The further observation that the different kinds of explicitly moral discourse in the New Testament are connected with those fundamental claims in various ways and degrees lends at least qualified support to the attempts of those who wish to distinguish different degrees of authority for different modes and levels of moral discourse.

Four Patterns of Moral Reasoning

In spite of the risk of oversimplification, it is instructive to examine a few of the patterns of argument that link explicit moral injunctions to the New Testament narrative and the theological claims derived from it. For illustrative purposes, I will define and give instances of four such patterns, examining in each case the closeness of the moral-theological connection and the character and specificity of the ethical demands being made. These examples are not understood to be either complete or mutually exclusive. They are offered only as a way to give content to the claim that the explicitly moral exhortations of the New Testament are tied to its central story and basic theological claims in a variety of ways and in differing degrees.

1. *Imitatio Dei*

A common New Testament pattern grounds the recommendation of moral ideals and behavior in emulation of the character of God or of Christ. From the breathtaking exhortation to "be perfect as your heavenly Father is perfect" (Mt. 5:48) to Paul's admonition to mutual forbearance, "Welcome one another therefore as Christ has welcomed you" (Rom. 15:7), we are called upon to imitate the divine love and mercy toward one another and all persons. In the Gospels, we find injunctions to forgiveness (Mt. 6:14-15 and par.), impartiality (Mt. 5:45 and par.), service (Mt. 20:27-28 and par.), self-sacrifice (Mt. 16:24 and par.), and love (Jn. 13:34), all explicitly based on the acts of God toward us or on the model of Christ's ministry among us. Similarly, in the epistles we find calls for humility and obedience (Phil. 2:3-12), kindness and forgiveness (Eph. 4:31–5:2), grounded in the example of Christ.

Here the link between moral principles and ideals and the basic narrative of the gospel is very close indeed, so that it is difficult to imagine how one could accept any of the substance of the New Testament account and not acknowledge the moral force of these claims upon one. The Christian's assent to them is the direct result of her awareness of the debt in which she stands and the free expression of her love for God, which has been awakened by God's grace in Jesus Christ. Further, it is her own witness to the nature of the God who is love and to the final victory of grace in the world, which is so much the heart of the gospel's claim.

Two things are to be noted about these injunctions: the first is that as calls to imitate character, they do in fact operate at the post-ethical and ideal-principle levels rather than at the level of moral rules. The other is that they are nonetheless the most strenuous of all the New Testament's demands, and are immediately linked to imperatives as disconcertingly specific as "if anyone strikes you on the right cheek, turn to him the other also" or "take up your cross." It is the call to imitate God in Christ that leads to the imperatives to love your enemies and to lose your life.

2. *Requirements of Fellowship*

A second pattern of moral reasoning, related but distinct, is that which insists upon holiness and purity as indispensable to fellowship with a holy

God. It is crucial to understand that this is not so much a precondition for fellowship as it is part of its character. It is not exactly a rule that light and darkness have no union: it is rather more like a fact. Nevertheless, the normative force is clear and compelling. Again and again, in the language of possession ("you are not your own, you were bought with a price"), identification ("your bodies are members of Christ"), and indwelling ("God's temple is holy, and that temple you are"), believers are reminded that the new life with God into which they are called entails abstention from malice, greed, sexual immorality, and deceit. (E.g., I Cor. 6:9-11, Eph. 4:17-24, Col. 3:5-10, Heb. 12:12-17.)

Here, besides the call to imitate God's character, is also the issue of freedom and fitness for the union with God in Christ that the New Testament posits as the proper end of human life. Readers of the epistles are "one spirit with [Christ]" (I Cor. 6:17); they must not "grieve the Holy Spirit in whom we were sealed for the day of redemption" (Eph. 4:30); they have been "raised with Christ," and their lives are to reflect the truth that they are destined to "appear with Him in glory" (Col. 3:1, 4).

While still fairly general in their appeal, the principles enjoining holiness of life, even more than those exhorting the imitation of God's love and forgiveness, have clear and specific injunctions and prohibitions linked to them. To use the examples cited above, the nature of the "unrighteousness" that I Corinthians 6:9a declares incompatible with God's fellowship is specified by the remainder of the passage, which declares the exclusion of the "immoral, idolaters, adulterers, sexual perverts, thieves and drunkards" from the kingdom (I Cor. 6:9b-10).

The most general of these terms are in turn specified in this and other texts. "Immorality" (Greek πορνεία) is explicated to include sex with prostitutes (I Cor. 6:15-18), and in the deutero-Pauline epistles idolatry is said to include greed, covetousness, and love of money (Eph. 5:5, Col. 3:6, II Tim. 3:2). Similarly, the "renewal" and "new nature" commended in Ephesians 4:17-24 are immediately further specified by a wealth of particular commands, ranging from "let the thief no longer steal" (4:28) to "do not get drunk with wine" (5:18). Following the exhortation to "put off the old nature with its practices," Colossians presents a long list of specific behavior to avoid (Col. 3:5, 8), and Hebrews follows the climactic "our God is a consuming fire" (12:29) with injunctions to hospitality, care for the ill-treated, and sexual fidelity in marriage (13:2-4).

The very assumptive character of the movement from generalities to such specificity, along with the somewhat formulaic character of the virtue- and vice-lists, argues for the strength of the moral consensus linking ethical principles and moral rules that existed at the time of the writing of these portions of the New Testament. It is because of that consensus as to what particular rules were entailed by what principles that terms as general as "immorality" or "licentiousness" could be used meaningfully without detailed argument establishing their content. For these New Testament writers (if not always for their readers), the prohibition of adultery inheres in the command to "shun immorality" (I Cor. 6:18), as the injunction "do not lie to one another" (Col. 3:9) is implied in the general exhortation to "put off the old deceitful nature"; the concrete injunctions form part of the meaning of those phrases as they are used.[1] Thus the demand for holiness of life, which is powerfully rooted in the central New Testament theme of union with God as the ultimate human destiny, also has strong links with the concrete injunctions to truth telling, chastity, sobriety, and generosity.

3. Practical Specification of Moral Norms

A third pattern of movement from theological to moral claim may be called "practical specification of general norms." It involves specifying how fundamental moral ideals, principles, and norms are to be honored in particular questions and situations. This is commonest in the letters of Paul, and is exemplified in his explication of the principle of love for neighbor to include regard for the conscience of the brother or sister even when it is in error (Rom. 14:13-21, I Cor. 8:4-13).

Other cases include Paul's elaboration of the principle of fidelity in marriage to allow (but not require) separation from an unbelieving spouse

1. The argument is frequently made that the specifications of these principles in the virtue- and vice-lists reveals the source of their content as secular or merely traditional, with the implication that these conventions have no "religious" content and are not binding upon us. Briefly, there is plenty of precedent for their content in the Old Testament, which the church claims as Scripture. Moreover, whatever the literary source for these norms, they are repeatedly drawn upon and given theological warrants in the New Testament, and must now be reckoned part of our own tradition. They may be treated critically and reevaluated in all the ways described as applicable to any moral rule, but no compelling argument has been made for dismissing them out of hand.

(I Cor. 7:12-16), as well as his advice concerning the preferability of the single state (I Cor. 7:25-38). Here explicitly it is the requirement of undivided devotion to God that is at issue, and the recommendation of celibacy is based upon practical considerations of distraction and impending difficulty (vv. 26, 28b, 34-35). Similar in character are Paul's repeated calls for an offering for the famine-stricken church in Jerusalem as the appropriate expression in these circumstances of the love and unity that bind the churches (e.g., II Cor. 8–9).

Some instances may also be cited from the general epistles. James 2:1-9, for example, describes what the principle of impartiality requires in a congregation of mixed economic class, and I Peter 2:13–3:6 outlines the particular form the imitation of Christ's humility and meekness is to take for persons in particular social stations.

The underlying principles, ideals, or rules that are being specified in these texts are either established by the means described above or simply assumed as part of the basic moral background of believers. The writer of I Peter explicitly invokes the authority of Christ's example, while in Romans 14 Paul only states that if a believer is injured by what we do, we are no longer walking in love, and treats the force of that observation as self-evident.

This category thus represents a kind of second-order moral reasoning, in which specific norms of conduct are related to theological claims indirectly, by way of their relation to more general ethical principles or ideals of character, like love of neighbor or humility. In this it resembles somewhat the pattern of argument we have already seen linking general principles and particular norms relating to holiness of life, but now the connections are less immediate and much more specific to the situation. Now it is necessary to describe or explain the instantiation of the principle, for we are no longer dealing with rules that are virtually part of the definition of their corresponding principles.

Further, the moral judgments here often involve empirical claims or assessments of the consequences of particular acts on others. As such, they introduce elements of contingency and complexity that were not present in earlier patterns. The specific injunctions that are adumbrated in these passages can frequently be stated as the conclusion of a series of "if" clauses: for example, "if you have a brother or sister who believes an action is wrong, and if (s)he is likely to observe your behavior (arising from your own liberty of conscience) and be tempted to act against his/her own conscience, then it is wrong to act in that manner because it may injure your brother or sister." While the moral force of such an injunction remains, there is a great deal of room for differing judgments about the presence of those conditions, and therefore for different conclusions about the relevance of the rule.

It is possible in similar fashion to outline the circumstances that condition Paul's instruction about separation from an unbelieving marriage partner or his advice to the Corinthians to remain single. The principles of marital fidelity and unqualified devotion to God are universally and permanently binding; it is the specific recommendations of separation or celibacy that are contingent, offered as responses to particular situations and in a determinate cultural context.

The passages from James and I Peter raise an analogous set of questions in that they assume a great deal about social structure and social relations, which makes their application in markedly different circumstances debatable. As above, the injunctions to impartiality and humility (both of which are grounded in the imitation of Christ) may be presumed always to apply; it is simply that Christians in our century cannot avoid partiality merely by refraining from making the poor sit on the floor, nor can their "subjection to every human institution" (I Peter 2:13) take the same form or have the same effect when the institutions themselves have changed so much.

In sum, the situational and cultural specificity that is natural to the process of specifying general principles in particular issues and cases is *part of* the moral reasoning of the New Testament in such passages, and to ignore that aspect of its argument is simply bad reading. Ironically, the tendency to ignore that specificity is one of the things held in common by those who wish to lift concrete rules out of their contexts and apply them flat-footedly no matter what the new situation and by those who wish to use the undesirability of so doing as a ground for dismissing *all* appeals to the text at the level of moral rule. Both strategies fail to attend to the ways in which particular circumstances, customs, and social structures may be woven into New Testament arguments about the appropriateness of specific rules.

Closer reading suggests that many of the New Testament's injunctions were never offered as timeless rules to be simply followed or rejected, but as examples of moral reasoning seeking to apply general principles to concrete cases. We can decide whether the outcomes of such reasoning are applicable in a new situation only by paying attention to the arguments that support them. Even where they are not applicable, such discussions remain useful to us in two ways. First, they underline the importance of the principles and ideals that particular judgments instantiate. Second, they provide examples of the process of moral discernment by which broad ideals of character and general principles of conduct are given concreteness and vitality.

4. Moral Prudence

The fourth and final pattern linking the central claims of the New Testament with ethical discourse bears some resemblance to that just discussed in that it concerns proper conduct in particular circumstances. However, in this case the conduct is not enjoined for the sake of a basic moral principle or even a stringent moral rule (as marriage can be recommended for the sake of avoiding immorality). Rather it is proposed as the best way to achieve some intermediate end (such as the unhindered preaching of the gospel or the avoidance of scandal or the maintenance of church discipline) that is judged important enough to warrant protection.

Examples of this pattern may be found in I Corinthians 9:19-22, where Paul describes himself as having "become all things to all persons" in order that nothing might deter those who heard his preaching, as well as in the arguments regarding the veiling of women (cf. especially I Cor. 11:4-7), which are based on the public dishonor done to the husband of a woman who prays without a veil, the symbol of his authority over her. The Corinthian passage enjoining the silence of women in worship (I Cor. 14:33-35) appears from its context to be motivated by a desire to avoid disorder and "indecency" in worship. Similar concerns ground the instruction of Titus 2:2-10: young men and old, older and younger women, slaves and Titus himself are given instructions geared to their role and station, which they are to follow in order that the "word of God not be discredited" (2:5).

Because of the practical importance of such ends, and because of their relation to God's ultimate goal of saving all who will believe, such prescriptions still have considerable moral weight — but it must be observed that we are at yet a further remove from the core of New Testament faith. From the witness to and emulation of the character of God, from the requirements of fellowship with God, from the concrete enactment of fundamental moral principles in particular circumstances, we have moved into the realm of what might be called (without prejudice) "expediency." In the classical sense in which prudence is a moral virtue, we are concerned here with prudential considerations, judgments about what acts best serve our goals and what may hinder them.

In addition, we have introduced a new kind of ambiguity into the argument, for now it includes assessing the effect of certain kinds of behavior not just upon particular others, but on a whole group of unspecified others who might be edified or scandalized or misled by what we do. It is obvious that any such assessment will of necessity be partly conjectural, and must take into account the character, beliefs, and expectations of those others. It must therefore be subject to change and revision as culture and history change the ways in which outsiders perceive and judge conduct. To use an example of conduct cited above, there is scant likelihood that any contemporary inquirer into Christian faith is going to be scandalized by women participating in worship without veils. In fact, such an inquirer is more likely to be scandalized by the continued marginalization of women in roles of church leadership, and to be prevented by their sense of moral offense from coming to faith.

It should be repeated at this point that these patterns of moral argumentation taken from the New Testament are not intended to be exhaustive, and it is acknowledged that they are frequently woven together in a single text. They are rehearsed here for the sake of illustration, to give some specificity to the contention that moral argument in the New Testament takes various forms, and that its norms are given varying degrees of force and situational particularity within the text. They demonstrate that not all practical imperatives are there presented as general moral rules, nor are they all related to the crucial claims about God's action in Christ in the same way or degree. If the further claim is accepted that the contemporary moral authority of Scripture for the church arises from that relationship, some substantial degree of guidance is provided to our attempts to understand and to weigh the force and relevance of the concrete directives of the New Testament for contemporary Christians.

Thus far we have dealt in general terms with the variety of linkages established in the New Testament between narrative accounts or theological claims and moral demands for conformity to certain principles and rules. While this may be thought sufficient to justify a case-by-case treatment of the weight of particular moral injunctions, it does not yet give us all the tools we might hope for in our analysis of the nature and force of moral claims in particular New Testament texts. A particularly illuminating framework for examining the context and structure of moral appeals in the New Testament is provided in the work of Wayne Meeks, in his treatment of New Testament ethical texts as instruments of resocialization for converts to the early church.[2]

The New Testament as the Conveyor of a Moral World

It must be said at the outset that Meeks's work is not directed to the question of how New Testament texts may be used in the moral life of the contemporary church.[3] Instead, he is concerned with a historical reconstruction of how the texts functioned to create and reinforce new moral communities in their original context, with their original audiences. His is a kind of sociological study, an ethnographic description aimed at showing how New Testament moral teaching worked to form a distinctive moral reference group with a distinctive way of life. On the one hand, this leads him to consider the relation between New Testament moral discourse and that of the cultures in which it developed. On the other, he pays close attention to the assumptions that undergird that discourse and to the stories, the expectations, and the self-understandings to which it appeals in its effort to explain and recommend particular forms of conduct as appropriate for Christians.

Despite its different agenda, this approach offers us benefits on two different levels. First, its attention to the implicit as well as the explicit foundations of moral discourse gives us additional tools with which to understand the ethical teaching of the New Testament. Second, this un-

2. *The Moral World of the First Christians* (Philadelphia: Westminster Press, 1986). This section also draws on unpublished material Meeks prepared for his 1988 graduate seminar, "Problems in Early Christian Ethics."

3. A possible exception is found in the brief but suggestive article "The Polyphonic Ethics of the Apostle Paul" (printed in the annual of the 1986 meeting of the Society of Christian Ethics). Here Meeks concludes a consideration of Paul's ethical method in two passages from I Corinthians and Romans with a few remarks about the hermeneutical implications of his work for our own appropriation of the New Testament in the doing of ethics.

derstanding in turn informs our normative judgments, as an appreciation for the original social context and function of moral instruction helps us to assess whether and how that instruction might continue to operate for the contemporary church.

Meeks proposes a number of questions as a starting point for describing early Christian ethics as they are revealed and inculcated by New Testament texts.[4] Some of these examine the explicit structure of the moral appeal, and correspond broadly to our earlier consideration of the various patterns of moral argument supporting particular norms of behavior. Other questions, which are of particular value for the present enterprise, are designed to elicit the implicit and generally unstated convictions and practices that form the social and symbolic world in which this moral discourse had its place. These are divided into four major areas, which I will summarize briefly.

1. *Perceived Behavior.* Just what were the things people were doing or were likely to do that the writer and/or audience regarded as morally significant? What relationships, perceptions, and the like make this a matter of moral importance? Do the writer and his readers share an assessment of this importance?
2. *Reference Groups.* Is the behavior being advocated or rejected referred either explicitly or implicitly to a particular group or social location? ("It is fitting for wives to obey" or "Do not behave like the Gentiles.") What is the relation between this positive or negative reference group and the dominant society? How is the moral behavior of other groups treated?
3. *Reality Perspectives.* In what kind of world do the moral appeals and the recommended behavior make sense? What aspects of this world are taken for granted? What aspects have to be asserted? What makes the things assumed in the appeal seem to the audience to be real in fact? Is God or are other transcendent realities invoked or necessarily assumed? To what extent do the moral norms depend upon some vision of a reality that will only become present in the future? What makes that future credible to the audience?
4. *Narrative.* Is a story told or assumed to be known as background or

4. This material is condensed and adapted from that prepared by Meeks for his 1988 graduate seminar, "Problems in Early Christian Ethics."

warrant for the moral appeal? If so, how does it function? Does it describe a reality of which we must take account? Or an action of God that sets us under obligation? How does the story connect with other elements described above? Does it render plausible an alternative account of reality? Provide warrants for identification with a particular reference group? Give a graphic portrayal of rewards and sanctions?

The Normative Usefulness of Sociological Description

The value of this work for our purposes lies first in the careful attention it pays to all the elements that together form moral understanding, and that give coherence, intelligibility, and significance to concrete ways of life. The range and delicacy of the questions proposed by Meeks guide our attention in a way that makes us better, more sensitive readers of the texts. They force us to look not only at what is explicitly said but at the implicit social and intellectual context in which these explicit appeals made sense: the "moral worlds" of their writers and readers.

Beyond the descriptive accuracy and completeness such an approach can foster, there are substantial benefits for interpretation. We cannot propose to uncover how some ancient instruction might (or might not) be applicable to our present situation if we have not understood why it was thought to be applicable to the situation it originally addressed. Conversely, that understanding can direct and clarify our efforts to weigh the force of moral instruction for the modern church by providing us with a range of questions that we must consider as part of our own movement from description to interpretation:

- Who was addressed, and what was assumed about the social situation they confronted? Do we occupy a similar situation?
- Why was the called-for behavior thought to have moral importance? Is the same behavior in our own time likely to have the same meaning or effect?
- What was assumed or asserted about reality, either historical or transcendent, that justified or required the conduct in question? Are we still prepared to assent to that view of reality, or has historical change and increased information made that view untenable?

Such questions are especially important in the assessment of instruction that falls into one of our two latter categories: those that are related to theological claims indirectly as specifications of more general principles and ideals, and those that we have characterized as the dictates of moral prudence. Precisely because of its specificity, instruction of this type often relies on a particular context of ideas and practices that justify and give moral significance to conduct. However, this reliance may be completely unspoken, part of the taken-for-granted intellectual and cultural context of writers and readers. By focusing on the place of ethical teaching in the moral world in which it arises, we gain insight into what was at stake in particular moral teachings and into the moral significance of the conduct that was approved or condemned, commanded or forbidden.

Meeks's questions remind us that behavior has its place and its meaning in a context of social structures and practices, beliefs and ideas, that inform the moral meaning of actions as surely as grammar and usage inform the meaning of words. In so doing, they offer us direction as we try to discern what claim particular injunctions have upon us, or what alternative conduct might evidence and sustain those loyalties and convictions we have in common with the writers and readers of these ancient texts.

Methodological Conclusions

I want at this point to summarize the arguments and observations contained in this chapter, and lay out clearly their consequences for a method of using the New Testament in constructive ethics. Not all of what follows will be novel, by any means; some of it is no more than common-sense observations about the necessity for thoroughness and attention to detail on the one hand and an appropriate degree of humility in making normative judgments on the other. Much of the rest builds upon the work of the other writers we have considered. Nonetheless, I believe it offers some positive advances on the work that has gone before, both in the form of needed specifications of general principles and in the form of critical revisions of methodological principles that have been seen to be faulty or problematic in their application.

Canonical Completeness

First and obviously, any effort to formulate general statements about New Testament norms in regard to a particular topic must take account of all the texts in its canon that might be thought relevant.

This commonplace (though frequently ignored) observation needs to be specified by two points. First, the unanimity of the New Testament's texts (or its lack) must be factored into the weight and certainty of any particular judgment. Second, the degree of attention given to an issue in the New Testament must guide the interpretation of texts concerning it. (It is dubious at best to take a rule cited once and in passing and exalt it into a major moral principle to be honored for all time.)

The next principle is a corollary of this first.

Dealing with Conflicts

Any substantial divergences between texts must be acknowledged and dealt with, either by showing how different norms were held to apply because of relevant differences in situation or by candid and reasoned judgments about what must take precedence.

The task of adjudicating conflicts between texts within the New Testament canon cannot be avoided or rendered innocuous by any trick of methodology. Such judgments remain complex and delicate, and we have no foolproof method for moral discernment. However, neither are we left entirely to our own devices, so that we must throw up our hands and declare the diversity of the New Testament an insurmountable obstacle to its ethical appropriation.

The suggestions of Birch and Rasmussen and others that the moral injunctions of Scripture be granted authority on a diminishing scale as one descends from more general ideals and goals to concrete and specific rules of practice begin to address this problem. So do the distinctions made by Allen Verhey in terms of the level of moral discourse that is addressed in particular passages. At the same time, we have seen that the position that the level of moral discourse simply determines whether or not ethical material can authorize moral judgments causes significant losses. It both blurs important and ethically useful distinctions between texts at the moral-rule level and impoverishes the material at the ideal-principle level, which we wish to employ.

Instead, attention must be paid to the actual moral arguments that ground and justify particular appeals at the level of moral rule and to the connection that is drawn between a rule and those theological or narrative claims to which we assent as Christians. We must examine the function of any rule in its multiple literary, theological, and historical contexts to see how and why it is taken to specify a broader principle, or serve an important goal, or instantiate a more universal demand to "lead a life worthy of the gospel."

The Uses and Limits of Rules

I propose that we grant concrete rules a degree of presumptive force that is not absolute, but may be overridden in particular circumstances.

If it seems clear that we cannot simply mechanically apply every imperative as a binding moral rule, it also seems clear that we cannot treat every appeal at the level of moral rule as uniform, or uniformly irrelevant. Rules of conduct may have to be discarded because the arguments for them are based on untenable treatments of Scripture; because they assume social structures that are vanished or different; because they conflict with principles they are supposed to embody; or because circumstances have shifted so that the goals they are proposed to serve are no longer served by them in fact. Arguments for particular judgments may also be rendered invalid by increases in empirical information.

In cases where such invalidation has occurred, we must make an effort to reweave the argument using our new data or changed historical circumstance. Particular injunctions may be overridden because of judgments about the consequences of some action in our changed circumstances or because of conflict with more fundamental biblical ideals, rules, or principles. In cases of conflict between texts at different levels of moral or theological generality and universality, higher levels of discourse may be said to "trump": to say that rules have presumptive weight is simply to say that the burden of proof is upon the one who wishes to discard some particular injunction or declare it irrelevant to our situation.

Recognizing the "Moral World"

In assessing the meaning and contemporary application of New Testament moral instruction, we must become aware of the implicit and largely unspoken assumptions that undergird that instruction, the "moral world" of which it formed a part.

Thus far I have stressed the necessity of attending to the moral arguments of the New Testament before we make a decision regarding the force or applicability of any particular moral teaching for us. Further refinement is provided if we employ the questions Meeks suggested, and examine not only the explicit moral arguments but the social and ideological context in which they made sense.

Here we focus on the place of any kind of moral instruction in the historical reality in which it was proposed, and the ways in which it presupposes a fabric of ideas and practices, whether as conventions to be supported or as adversaries to be opposed. By bringing these background assumptions into view, we can evaluate whether we can and do inhabit a world in which this teaching continues to "make sense" and where this conduct can witness to and sustain the commitments we have in common despite the centuries. This is particularly useful where the patterns of moral argument grounding specific norms correspond to those we have called "practical application" or "moral prudence," which may rely on unspoken assumptions about the social meaning of behavior for their force.

Finally, by looking at how these texts sought to reorder loyalties and reshape conduct into that appropriate to a distinctively Christian community, we gain a number of useful insights into problems that continue to trouble the modern church. What is to be our relation to the moral assumptions of the dominant (in our case, secular) society? To what extent can they be modified or reinterpreted to accord with Christian profession, and to what extent must they be directly challenged or simply rejected? What effect does the eschatological horizon of Christian belief have on the assessment of mundane social structures and relationships, and how is the Christian to sustain a coherent moral life in the already-but-not-yet of existence "between the times"? Questions like these will become increasingly relevant as any actual Christian community seeks to move beyond description and interpretation of the ethical content of the New Testament into moral self-criticism and decision making.

The Limits of Methodology

Method may not be separated from exegesis; it must be nuanced and informed by continued conversation with the canon it seeks to interpret.

Perhaps the central contention here is that as there is no uniformity in the moral instruction of the New Testament, no principles of method for its use can be established in isolation from the actual reading of actual texts. Precisely because the New Testament is not uniform, sweeping judgments about its situational specificity and cultural limitations rendering it unable to authorize any particular moral judgments cannot be sustained. Neither can generalizations about the irrelevance of address at particular levels of moral discourse be made without any attention to the diversity of foundations for what might be called "moral rules" in the New Testament.

Not that this proposal is to be understood as denying the force or the importance of the issues raised by those thinkers we considered. It accepts the diversity and even the inconsistency of the Christian canon emphasized by Gustafson without concluding that the moral authority of Scripture is thereby forfeited, and it suggests some particular lines of argument to be pursued in weighing the relative force of disparate texts. It welcomes the distinctions in moral authority granted to different kinds of New Testament discourse by Birch and Rasmussen and Verhey, and sees this as an apt reflection of the fact that Christian allegiance to that canon is in the first instance theological rather than ethical. It presents a number of circumstances in which extrabiblical sources of insight and information or historical changes may be taken to overrule or invalidate the moral arguments of the New Testament and the conclusions they warrant. But in all these cases the emphasis is on the particularities of the biblical material itself: the way in which its ethical instruction is (or is not) rooted in the central affirmations of the New Testament canon; the degree of situational specificity internal to its argument; the importance of historical circumstances in shaping its concrete admonitions. These considerations must guide our assessment of the moral relevance and applicability of its teaching to our own lives. And these must be evaluated patiently, painstakingly, one text at a time.

This proposal, of course, does not solve every possible problem. It does not provide an airtight method for evaluating every moral rule or avoiding every perilous and difficult moral judgment. What of the cases where the grounds for moral rules are not clearly provided in the text or are unintelligible, or where the conflict is with deeply felt moral intuitions that seem not to have occurred to the biblical writers at all? How is the church to adjudicate conflicts between two rules or principles that seem equally well or poorly founded, and how can it maintain church unity in all the cases where there is room for a diversity of responsible moral judgments? At another level, how can the church and its people learn to shed the blinders of their own moral failings and let the Bible speak to them a word that is new and that can genuinely stand over against them as God's own?

In short, there is no substitute for moral wisdom, nor any proof against moral failure. Nevertheless, I will maintain that the church has a great deal to learn from careful and disciplined attention to the whole range of New Testament moral instruction, in all of its historical and ideological situatedness. But such assertions mean little; the test of this or any ethical method lies in its fruitfulness in application, in the extent to which it can illuminate the texts we consider and advance the moral inquiries we put to it.

CHAPTER 3

Mark 10:17-31

Preliminary Questions

My earlier stress on the need to take into account the situation of the original writers and readers in the interpretation of ethical material in the New Testament makes it natural to wonder about the community Mark had in mind when he wrote his Gospel. Who and where were these people? What was the composition of their group? What was the situation of the early church that prompted the creation of this distinctive literary genre, the Gospel? All of these are interesting questions, and ones whose answers might in fact be invaluable. The difficulty is that their answers remain in dispute. The traditional view of the date and location of Mark's Gospel places it in Rome in the decade 65 to 75 C.E.[1] Members of this school see the gospel as addressed to the confrontation with Roman society and with persecution. Recent scholarship has challenged this view, hypothesizing instead that Mark was addressed to the Palestinian Christian community concerned about the delay of the Parousia.[2]

1. Commentators who hold this view rely on the early testimony of Papias cited by Eusebius (*Hist. Eccl.,* III xxxix), on the second century Anti-Marcionite Prologue to the Gospels, and on a reference of Irenaeus (*Adv. Haer.,* III 1.2.) to attribute the Gospel to an interpreter of Peter writing shortly after the apostle's death. Recent interpreters who hold to this view include William Lane, Martin Hengel, Ernest Best, and Donald Senior.

2. For the classic expression of this view, see W. Marxsen's monograph, *Mark the Evangelist: Studies on the Redaction-History of the Gospel* in the English translation (Nashville: Abingdon Press, 1969). Scholars who incline to some version of this theory include Werner Kelber, Howard Kee, and Ched Myers, in his recent *Binding the Strong Man: A Political Reading of Mark's Gospel* (New York: Orbis, 1985).

Whatever we might desire to know, at present we can only offer more or less persuasive conjecture, and in fact I do not find the evidence for either of these efforts at historical reconstruction compelling.[3] As much as might be gained by greater clarity about the original situation, our interest in the ethical appropriation of the passage found in the canon does not strictly require that it be identified in any detail or with great certainty. Thus the emphasis in my own interpretation will fall on the literary rather than on the historical context of Mark's story: that is, the narrated setting and situation as the text presents it, and the place the passage is given within the canonical Gospel of Mark. In that restricted sense, the setting and situation of Mark 10:17-31 is on the road to Jerusalem shortly after Jesus' first two predictions of his death and immediately before the third. The narrated audience[4] is first the unidentified man and later the group of disciples, who apparently witness the encounter between the man and Jesus and continue to question him about what they have heard.

The passage is placed within Mark's Gospel shortly after the midpoint occupied by Peter's confession. It reflects the shift from a narrative dominated by events — geographical movement, miracles, the calling and commissioning of disciples — to one in which dialogue, preaching, and teaching take center stage. It is to these visible features of the narrative that we will look to provide us with clues in its interpretation.[5]

Translation

Considering the various and ingenious efforts of commentators ancient and modern to find an alternative to the apparent plain sense of this

3. Although I am somewhat inclined to favor a Roman provenance, in light of the antiquity of that ascription.

4. That is, those persons identified or implied to be present by the story's plot.

5. This general approach to the task of interpreting Mark is shared by other commentators with constructive ethical and theological interests. See M. A. Tolbert, *Sowing the Gospel: Mark's World in Literary-Historical Perspective* (Minneapolis: Fortress Press, 1989) and especially Dan O. Via, Jr.'s literary critical study focusing on Mark 10, *The Ethics of Mark's Gospel — In the Middle of Time* (Philadelphia: Fortress Press, 1985). He gives a brief but interesting defense of moving from descriptive to normative ethical interests rooted in W. Iser's reader-response criticism (pp. 3-5). Despite his other commitments, Myers *(Binding the Strong Man)* is also attentive to the hermeneutical cues of literary form, structure, and context.

passage, the manuscript tradition has remarkably few significant variants.[6] In all the cases where there is some variant, scholars generally agree as to the preferable reading.

The translation that follows is of the Greek text as presented in the third edition of the United Bible Societies' Greek New Testament.[7] It is literal to a fault, preserving the repetitiousness and the awkwardness of certain phrases, preserving even the word order of the Greek within the limits of English grammar. My aim is simply to give the flattest possible rendering of Mark's text, so that the English reader has an opportunity to be confronted by the bluntness of this rather surprising story.

17 And as he was going out into the way, one came running up and, kneeling to him, said to him, "Good Teacher, what must I do in order to inherit eternal life?"

18 And Jesus said to him, "Why do you call me 'good'? No one is good but one — God.

19 The commandments you know: Do not kill, do not commit adultery, do not steal, do not witness falsely, do not defraud, honor your father and your mother."

20 But he said to him, "Teacher, all these things I have kept from my youth."

21 And Jesus looking hard at him loved him, and said, "One thing is lacking to you: whatever things you have, sell, and give [to the] poor, and you will have treasure in heaven, and come follow me."

22 But he was appalled[8] at the word, and went away grieving, for he had many possessions.

6. Some manuscripts, as well as the parallel passages in Matthew and Luke, omit the words μή ἀποστερήσῃς ("do not defraud") from verse 19 as improper in a list of citations from the Decalogue, and the Western text transposes verses 24 and 25 to create a more logical progression. The other variants that do appear are chiefly in verses 24 and 25, and appear to be efforts on the part of copyists to make the passage seem less extreme. For example, in verse 25, κάμηλον (camel) is changed to κάμιλον (rope or hawser) in several manuscripts, apparently so the analogy will no longer be absurd but merely impossible!

7. Kurt Aland, Matthew Black, Carlo M. Martini, Bruce Metzger and Allen Wikgren, eds. American edition published by United Bible Societies, New York, 1975.

8. This is offered as the first definition of the participle στυγνάσας in Walter Bauer,

23 And looking around, Jesus said to his disciples, "How hard it will be for those having riches to enter into the kingdom of God!"
24 And the disciples were astounded at his words. And Jesus answering said again to them, "Children, how hard it is to enter into the kingdom of God;
25 it is easier [for] a camel to pass through the eye of a needle than [for] a rich man to enter into the kingdom of God."
26 But they were exceedingly astonished, saying to themselves, "And who can be saved?"
27 Looking hard at them Jesus said, "With men [it is] impossible, but not with God. For all things are possible with God."

28 Peter began to say to him, "Look, we have left all things and have followed you."
29 Jesus said: "Truly I tell you, there is no one who left house or brothers or sisters or mother or father or children or fields for the sake of me and for the sake of the gospel, [30] but he receives a hundredfold, now in this time, houses and brothers and sisters and mothers and children and fields, with persecutions, and in the coming age, eternal life.
31 And many first will be last, and the last first."

The paragraphing above reflects the fact that the passage breaks rather neatly into three parts, all defined by distinct conversations with distinct partners. A fair amount of literature argues for the original independence of these parts of the text, and speculates on their earlier forms and sources.[9]

At the same time, strong internal evidence indicates that the association of these passages in the canonical text is reflective and deliberate

---

William F. Arndt, F. Wilbur Gingrich, and Frederick Danker, *A Greek-English Lexicon of the New Testament and Other Early Christian Literature,* 2nd ed. (Chicago: University of Chicago Press, 1979) and explicitly as a possible translation of Mk 10:22. I choose it here because the suggestion of shock accords well with the recorded reaction of the disciples, who are "astounded" (ἐθαμβοῦντο) at Jesus' teaching. I find it interesting that not a single translation I could find took this option, although the NRSV comes closest with "shocked."

9. For the most extensive discussion, see Ernest Best, *Disciples and Discipleship: Studies in the Gospel According to Mark* (Edinburgh: T & T Clark, 1986).

on the redactor's part. The narrative connection between the conversation with the unidentified man and that with the disciples is clear, as the latter provides both an emphasis and interpretation for the former. Despite the rather looser connection between 17-27 and 28-31, there is a powerful indication that Mark at least intends them to be read together; only in verse 30 do we return to the question posed in verse 17. Shifting from his more usual phrase βασιλείαν τοῦ θεοῦ ("the kingdom of God," vv. 24-25), Jesus here promises the eschatological reward of discipleship using the term of his original interlocutor, ζωὴν αἰώνιον ("life eternal"). I will focus on the passage in its present form of three related parts; this does not imply any particular judgment on the question of the text's prehistory.

Reading the Story

I have already argued that understanding the ethical significance of a passage requires attention to the logic internal to its teaching. In the case of discursive parenetic texts, this means attending to the explicit argument supporting a particular injunction and to the underlying assumptions that form the background of that argument. But in cases like the present, where imperatives are set within a story, it means in the first instance simply paying close attention to that story. We must follow the narrative movement of the passage, and examine the function of the explicitly moral discourse within its narrative setting and within the larger narrative of the Gospel where it has its place.

Accordingly, I begin this section of the chapter by tracing the development of the passage through each of its three parts. I will go on to consider the relation between the passage as a whole and the Gospel of Mark, and how that is conveyed by its place in the structure of the Gospel. This will give us grounds for a descriptive account of the original moral content and significance of the text.

In the final section I will consider the background assumptions and implicit structures, the "moral world" within which the discourse takes place and has its force. Then we will be in a position to make further judgments about whether and how that content might be thought to apply in another time, place, and situation: that of the contemporary Christian church.

Verses 17-22

To begin, it is worth noting what is *not* in the story, which is any of the specific information that has led to the traditional reference to this passage as "the story of the rich young man" or alternatively "of the rich ruler." These details are, of course, borrowed from the parallel texts in Matthew 19 and Luke 18. In Mark, the minimalist εἷς ("one") which begins the story is never supplemented by any detail other than that provided in the final clause, which asserts, "he had many possessions." The use of masculine pronouns identifies the speaker as male, but he is never so much as called a man, much less a young man or a ruler. Beyond the fact of his ownership revealed at the very end, we know nothing about him except what can be inferred from his recorded words and actions. Mark by his reticence makes the man a neutral figure, a figure of "Everyman" who shares his lot as an owner of many possessions.

The passage begins, as so many in Mark, with the abruptness of urgency. The man comes to Jesus at a dead run and kneels in front of him on the road, launching the conversation with a form of address as remarkable as his question: "Good Teacher." Jesus (somewhat to the embarrassment of the church) repudiates the title "Good," referring the man instantly to the God who alone is good. In keeping with this perfectly orthodox response, Jesus goes on to give the only answer a rabbi[10] could give to one who asks the way to life: he refers the man to the law. Moreover, the form of his answer unites him to his questioner in the same way as his refusal to be called good. The commandments are what they both "know," and the commandments stand outside both of them as the Way to life.

But the man will not leave it at that. If he is not sure that he has life, yet he is sure of his keeping of the law, and Jesus does not challenge his claim to have kept the commandments from his youth. It is in this very confidence that Jesus finds occasion, as Mark notes, to love him, and to reveal to him what single thing he lacks. He tells his questioner to sell

10. I generally agree with Via's observation that Mark is rather more concerned with Jesus' role as a teacher than is usually acknowledged (*Ethics of Mark's Gospel*, p. 69), even if not with the remark he cites from Achtemeier that Mark regards this as "an adequate Christological role" (ibid., see note). Jesus is in this passage, among other things, the Teacher who answers the question put to him, though his "teaching" does and must take the form "follow me."

whatever he possesses and follow Jesus himself — the one whom he has known enough to call Good, and known enough to ask for eternal life. It is as if Jesus turns from the second table of the Decalogue, which he has quoted, to the first: to the command to love God with a united heart, which alone gives intelligibility and meaning to all that follows. And for this man in this moment, as always and everywhere in Mark's Gospel, the form that love of God takes *is* discipleship. Alongside the law as the Way of life, Jesus offers him the way on which they stand, the road to Jerusalem that Jesus follows to his own fate, as the Way to life.

This offer and the man's response to it form the hinge on which the whole story turns. Up until now, the arrested momentum of Jesus' own movement and the urgency and fervor of his interlocutor all carry us forward toward the one end that is already in view: the end that Jesus has twice described, and that he will describe still more vividly in the pericope that immediately follows. The reader who has followed Mark this far *knows* that the man must follow Jesus on this road, that this is the answer to his question. But unexpectedly the direction of the story's movement is reversed. In this moment, and perhaps never before, the man realizes that he cannot go. He is appalled at the word (v. 22; see my note 8, p. 41). *Because his possessions are many,* as the causal connective γαρ of verse 22 tells us, he is unable to leave them even to have the life he knows enough to seek. And remarkably, even here — in the act of this single recorded refusal of discipleship in all the Gospels[11] — the man also knows enough to sorrow for the life he is foregoing. He departs grieving, the text tells us: the first to mourn his own death.[12]

It is a stunning story. So much so that nearly every commentator feels constrained to point out that it *is* a story, the record of a particular encounter with a particular individual, and not a programmatic statement of Jesus about the ethics of property ownership. This is a valid and important observation, but its precise import is not self-evident. Many of the same commentators go on to assert something to the effect that Jesus' rigor in this case was the result of something he perceived (supernaturally,

11. Taking this story with its parallels in Matthew and Luke as versions of one recollection.

12. Cf. Via, *Ethics of Mark's Gospel,* p. 138: "Riches deceive in the precise sense that they seduce one into believing that life can be found in them. . . . And yet one *knows* that he is letting himself be deceived, otherwise why would the man have gone away sorrowing?"

one supposes) about the state of this particular rich man's soul. Not only was this man rich, goes the argument, but he loved or trusted or was otherwise unduly attached to his wealth, so that in this case (and not presumably in others) the surrender of his property was necessary. For this rich man, wealth was an obstacle to faithfulness to God's call in a way that it might not be to another. That there is a kernel of truth in this analysis, I will not deny. What problems it presents as a reading of this text become clear as soon as one continues the narrative.

Verses 23-27

No sooner has the man gone from the scene than Jesus widens the scope of the conversation just ended by asserting as a generality what has been enacted in the individual case. Mark emphasizes the inclusion of all the disciples with the introductory περιβλεψάμενος, and underlines the force of the assertion with the exclamatory πῶς: "How hard it will be for those having riches to enter into the kingdom of God!" (v. 23). That this is an extraordinary, even a shocking, thing to say may be inferred from the reaction recorded for the disciples. They are "astounded" (v. 24 — ἐθαμβοῦντο) at his word, even as the man was appalled at the word that called him to give away his possessions.

If their amazement is understandable in view of the traditional identification of almsgiving, fasting, and prayer (all directly or indirectly facilitated by wealth) as the works of Jewish piety, still Jesus does not linger to explain the point. In repetition, the exclamation is rendered more general yet: "Children, how hard it is to enter into the kingdom of God!" (v. 24). Lest this expansion seem to weaken the focus on the particular problem of riches, Jesus here draws the analogy about camels going through the eyes of needles more easily than the rich into the kingdom (v. 26). Further, the text offers no reason to assume that Jesus' words are intended or understood as merry good humor or colorful Oriental exaggeration. At this point the disciples are described literally as "struck outside"[13] themselves (ἐξπλήσσοντο — v. 26) with astonishment, and the intensity of this reaction is itself a clue to the meaning

13. Max Zerwick and Mary Grosvener, *A Grammatical Analysis of the New Testament* (Rome: Biblical Institute Press, 1974), 1:141.

and weight of this story. In confusion they ask each other, "And who can be saved?"

This is the cue for the reintroduction of an idea from the preceding chapter of the Gospel, already hinted at by the address to the disciples as τέκνα ("children"; compare 10:15). Human helplessness in the face of the demands of the kingdom is acknowledged, but it is more than overcome by confidence in God's power. "All things are possible with God" (v. 27). Significantly, however, it is specifically power and not patience or mercy that is called upon here. There is nothing to suggest that God's call or its demands will be somehow softened or made more "reasonable" and more compatible with ordinary life: only that God can make possible — even for the rich — the wholehearted response that the kingdom requires. That this is the force of the passage is supported by the text that follows, particularly if one suspects that it is brought here from some other context to serve Mark's purpose.

Verses 28-31

"Look, we have left everything and have followed you" (v. 28). Peter's assertion, which seems so oddly self-congratulatory when viewed in isolation, becomes transparent as soon as it is considered in its place as the opening of this third vignette. From the cameo enactment of discipleship refused because of property, to the general warning of the nearly insuperable obstacle wealth presents, we move to the corresponding enactment of the call heard and obeyed — and to the conditions under which that obedience is rendered.

Three things are especially noteworthy. First is that the form obedience takes explicitly includes both leaving and following. Second, the leaving referred to is not some kind of inner detachment of the soul from objects still in possession, but a perfectly literal departure from literal objects, places, and people. It is the concrete abandonment of one life for the sake of another. Finally, it is of more than passing importance that Peter speaks in the first person plural, as part of the group of disciples. While the one who refuses goes his way alone, to heed the call is to become one of the community of followers.

Perhaps this is what is meant by Jesus' somewhat puzzling response about the hundredfold recompense received "now in this time" by those who have left behind property and families for his sake and the gospel's (vv. 29-30). What is received is the community of those who follow, more extensive and more vital than natural communities and the social and property structures on which they depend. That there is some tension between this assertion and the conditions under which the disciples can expect to live is indicated by the awkward appending of the phrase μετὰ διογμῶν ("with persecutions" — v. 30). Whatever the real richness of life in community, it is experienced, against the background of persecutions, as permanently insecure. By his reuse of the phrase "for my sake and the sake of the gospel," Mark subtly reminds the reader of the other occasion when a recompense is promised for the losses incurred in discipleship: the text in 8:35 that promises "whoever will lose his life . . . will save it." Only "the age which is coming" provides the outer horizon that makes discipleship a reasonable course, and with it the looked-for "life eternal" with which the story began.[14]

We have thus come full circle to see how the passage as a whole provides what is for Mark the only possible answer to the question posed at the outset: what is the way to eternal life? The answer given by the law is neither wrong nor incomplete: to love God with the whole heart is the substance both of obedience and of readiness for the kingdom. But for Mark this undivided love is identical with following Jesus on the road to

14. This, along with the continual reference to Jesus' death (see below) is what convinces me that Mark's eschatology must be taken in *some* way that can transcend the claims of life and the fear of death in order for his ethical stance to retain its rational force and its status as "action-guide." There must be an aspect of the Kingdom in its futurity that is transcendent and/or transhistorical in order for the underlying "lose your life to save it" to make sense.

This still leaves room for important and substantive disagreements both in the exegesis of Mark and in constructive theological understandings of eschatology; I question, though, whether it leaves enough room for what Via calls the "demythologized" version of eschatology that he assumes is necessary to "make [apocalyptic] available immediately for use in contemporary ethical reflection" (*Ethics of Mark's Gospel*, p. 7). Via's defense of the "happy ending" of Mark's gospel constituted by Jesus' resurrection and promised return is curiously qualified, defending on the one hand the "subjective transcendence of an unchanged tragic world" and on the other "hope for movements toward the improvement of the human social community in history" (p. 37). Via acknowledges the "mythological" aspect of Mark's story, its appeal to an angelic visitation and an empty tomb (however its narration is compromised by the fear and silence of the women to whom the revelation is given). But he often speaks as if this ground of ethical action in Mark is dispensable. In short, I do not think it is.

Jerusalem, and thus the way to life is first a way to death; it is a journey on which there can be no provision for baggage. The costs are appalling, paid in severed human relationships as well as in silver, and the capacity to bear them is the work of God and not of human beings. While the present rewards of the journey are real and rich, they are also vulnerable; only under the eschatological horizon is this way revealed unambiguously as the road to life.

The closing line of the passage concerning the first and the last harkens back to a similar inversion from an earlier chapter (9:35), and provides the occasion to examine the place of this text within the larger narrative of Mark's Gospel.

Place in the Structure of Mark

I have already referred to the commonplace observation that Mark's Gospel is structured around a midpoint occupied by Peter's confession. Broadly speaking, the first half of Mark's Gospel may be said to concern the establishment of Jesus' identity as Messiah. Beginning with the superscription "the beginning of the gospel of Jesus Christ," it turns immediately to the preaching of John the Baptist concerning the one who is to come after him (1:7-8), and reaches forward in a long arch to the declaration "You are the Christ" (8:29).

But if the disciples there have "the right answer," Mark is quick to indicate that they don't know what it means. No sooner are these words out of Peter's mouth than Jesus warns the disciples to tell no one, and the narrative takes an abrupt turn as Jesus begins to teach that he must die (8:31). The second half of the Gospel (8:31–16:8 [or :20]) is occupied with Mark's account of what it means for Jesus to be the Christ, and it is dominated by the long narrative of the passion week that fills chapters 11 to 16.

In between the climactic confession of 8:29 and the entrance to Jerusalem that marks the beginning of the passion narrative in 11:1, a series of events and pronouncements focus on who Jesus is, and particularly on what it means to follow him. It begins as I have indicated, with Jesus' declaration that the Son of Man must suffer (8:31). Peter's shocked protest is repudiated in the most extreme terms (8:33), and Jesus delivers the first and controlling characterization of discipleship: it is taking up the cross to follow him (8:34). The transfiguration narrative that follows serves to confirm Jesus' identity and his teaching authority (9:2-8). The pair of healing miracles of 9:14-29 and 10:46-52[15] provide a dramatic enactment of those who have ears to hear and eyes to see, and form a literary frame within which a series of teachings on discipleship and the demands of the kingdom is organized.[16]

This is the structure within which our passage takes its place, as part of the exposition of what following Jesus means and requires.[17] Two recurrent themes punctuate this exposition. The first of these is the constant threnody of Jesus' coming suffering and death (8:31, 9:9, 9:12, 9:31, 10:33-34, 10:38; 10:45). The second is the series of paradoxes and reversals that assert in a variety of ways that among the followers of Jesus, greatness belongs to those who are of least account: those who are last; who are smallest; who serve; who receive what they have no status to claim (9:35-37, 10:14-15, 10:31, 10:43-44). Nor are these reversals arbitrary, merely a sort of poetic critique of social structures. As the closing pronouncement of the section indicates, lowliness and self-denial are the pattern of discipleship *because* Jesus' serving takes the form of giving his life (10:43-45).

Our particular passage is placed squarely between statements of these two themes. It is preceded by Jesus' assertion that one who does not receive

15. In addition, as many commentators, including Myers, Via, and Tolbert, have pointed out, the healing of Bartimaeus provides a match for the healing of the blind man in 8:22-36. These two restorations of sight form the narrative frame that encloses the three predictions of the passion, as well as a contrast to the lack of understanding and insight displayed by the disciples.

16. The broad outline of the structure of Mark given in this paragraph corresponds in its general features to that proposed by Ched Myers (*Binding the Strong Man,* pp. 235-89), to whom I am in debt for the observation about the literary function of the pair of healing miracles in 9:14ff. and 10:46ff. (at 238). While I sometimes find the particulars of his political/ethical analysis unpersuasive or even tendentious (cf. my note 20, p. 52) I often find Myers's attention to the literary structure of Mark very illuminating.

17. Via understands this chapter similarly as an exposition of discipleship, although his overall account is somewhat different. He understands Mark's gospel as the rendering of the apocalyptic end of the plot of the world's time, into the tripartite story of Jesus and his disciples (*Ethics of Mark's Gospel,* e.g., pp. 32ff. and 45-47). This chapter in Mark is for Via "the middle of the middle" (ibid., pp. 76-79), the densely packed center of this double-framed narrative, which "points both backward and forward, illuminating the whole" (p. 77). This has the effect of increasing the theological centrality of this text, and raising the ethical stakes higher still.

the kingdom of God as a child will never enter it at all, and followed by the longest and most vivid account of what awaits at the end of the road to Jerusalem. The rich man stands as a kind of antitype of discipleship because he is unable either to leave or to follow, and so he exemplifies the inverse of both of these themes. He cannot leave behind the power conferred by his possessions to become one who receives (which means paradoxically that he is in the power of his possessions); and he cannot travel on the road to Jerusalem, because he cannot give up the life he has even for the sake of the life he searches for.[18]

This context makes two things clear. The first is that, in light of Mark's insistence that discipleship is formally following Jesus on "the way of the cross," the idea that it might require something as drastic as poverty cannot be put aside as improbable or unreasonable.[19] The second is that the point is no more poverty than it is death. The central concern of Mark's Gospel is not wealth but discipleship, and the punchline of our story is not "whatever you have sell it" but rather "come follow me." It is important although dangerous to say here that the value of poverty for Mark is purely secondary and instrumental, as is the disvalue of wealth. For Mark, the fact of the man's wealth is the least important thing about him, deservedly tacked on at the end of the account as a kind of afterthought. Wealth has no importance at all except as a stumbling block — which is to say, it

18. In keeping with her understanding of the parable of the sower and its interpretation (4:3-32) as a sort of synopsis of Mark's gospel, Tolbert (*Sowing the Gospel*, p. 157) cites 10:17-22 as the preeminent example of the "seed sown among thorns." Interestingly, and rightly I think, she sees Herod (6:14-29) as the other instance of this type (pp. 157-58). While this is apt enough, I would take some issue with her account of the disciples as instancing only and simply the "seed sown on rocky ground." As she herself observes (pp. 209-10), it is the disciples' desire for other things such as glory and authority that constitutes their "hardness of heart," their blindness and deafness to the preaching of the Kingdom. Against her contention that the pattern of resistance to the gospel occasioned by the competing desires of the world is one that "was not overly interesting or relevant to the author" (p. 157), I would maintain that the categories represented in the parable are not as well defined and watertight in Mark as her analysis suggests; there is a reason why trials or losses are the occasion for the apostasy of those who fall away under persecution, a connection that is made explicitly later in this passage (see above, p. 47).

19. It is curious to see commentators struggle to explain how discipleship for Mark cannot really require poverty when they have already dealt fairly straightforwardly with Mark's view that discipleship may well entail martyrdom. It reminds one rather inescapably of the old joke about the man who, confronted by a robber with the demand, "Your money or your life," responded, "I'm thinking it over."

would have had no importance at all if it had not prevented him from following.[20]

The Moral Use of the Story

"Moral Worlds": The First Century's . . .

Before we go on to assess what moral import this passage might have for the contemporary church, it will help to flag for our own discussion what I have called (following Meeks) the "moral world" in which it operated: the social groups and their assumptions, ideas, and convictions that form the background or ideological subtext to the passage, and the setting in which its moral teaching made sense. In the previous chapter I identified four aspects of that world: perceived behavior (what acts are thought to have moral significance and why); reference groups (the implicit or explicit "we" that may operate behind a text to give moral norms a kind of purchase or claim on actual or would-be members of the group); reality perspective (the set of assumptions about what is real or true about the world, both mundane and transcendent); and narrative (the implicit or explicit story that operates as a context of interpretation). For the present text, all four of these aspects of the moral world may be seen to be operating in various ways. I will discuss them briefly in the order given.

"Perceived Behavior": The question, What behavior is perceived to have moral importance and why? is another version of the one we have just been discussing: What is the moral concern with the state of wealth? I have said that the context of our passage in the Gospel indicates that its

20. Contrast the reading of Myers, who, consistently with his overall approach, takes this text as concerned centrally with the repudiation of the man's class status as a landholder (*Binding the Strong Man,* pp. 273-74). Its point, he tells us, is that Jesus' ethic requires solidarity with the poor, and "the *only* way to salvation for the rich is by the redistribution of their wealth — that is, the eradication of class oppression" [his emphasis] (p. 275). Against such a reading, I would cite the relatively scant attention of the text to the claims of the poor (despite the inclusion of the "do not defraud"); its focus is on the issue of whether the man can follow and thus can find the Kingdom and enter eternal life, not on whether he is recruited to the side of the poor as such. Via (with obvious regret) reaches the same conclusion about this passage in his analysis of ethical intentions, motives, and consequences in Mark (*Ethics of Mark's Gospel,* pp. 82-84).

moral importance is secondary or derivative, arising entirely from its relation to Mark's primary (one might say single) concern with discipleship. The decisive weight of this passage falls on wealth's feature of being a potential obstacle to discipleship, rather than on the need to give to the poor or the possibility of having treasure in heaven.[21] To put it another way, it is not the state of being wealthy that is in question, but the fatal state of being unable to abandon wealth to follow Jesus. We will return to consider what this suggests about the normative use of this passage for the contemporary church.

"Reference Groups": We may speak of two different reference groups within the storied world of Mark's narrative. There is the implicit "we," which includes Jesus' interlocutor and all those who may be assumed to know the commandments of the Decalogue and their positive relation to the sought after "eternal life" (v. 19). (Notably, this group also includes both Jesus and the disciples.) There is also the explicit "we" of Peter's assertion, those who have "left everything and followed you" (v. 28). This includes only the disciples out of the world of the story.

"Reality Perspective": It is surprising and important to note that these two groups, which are separated so crucially from one another by their following Jesus or failing to, are in fact united to a great extent by what we have called their "reality perspectives." They share a social identity and a history of interpretation gathered around Torah. They thus share a common theological and moral vocabulary broad enough to make sense of the question about "eternal life" and of Jesus' response insofar as it is couched in terms of the law, or even of the "kingdom of God." More broadly, they share an account of reality in which transcendent claims and eschatological gains and losses ("eternal life") can have force and credibility.

Within the world of Mark's story, it is more difficult to state what it is that separates the disciples from the man who confronts Jesus on the street. It is not clearly knowledge, or even faith (the disciples' knowledge and faith are notoriously weak in Mark); it is not courage (all the disciples variously betray, deny, and abandon Jesus to his fate in the end). All the story tells us is that the man goes away mourning *because* his possessions are great. Here the property that is of no importance becomes absolutely central, as its possession seems to paralyze him, so that he cannot make

21. In this respect contrast Luke's text in 12:22-34 (which we take up in the next chapter) where there *is* an emphasis on having one's treasure in heaven.

even the stumbling and fitful start on the way that characterizes Mark's disciples. Perhaps it gives the man a stake in the world-as-it-is too great to throw in his lot with the "age which is coming," so that he is imprisoned by his ties to the present order. A certain stubborn opacity to the story reduces us to saying simply that the difference between the group of disciples and the unidentified man is the fact that the man refuses to follow.

One way in which this text would have operated morally for Mark's original readership is by including in the group of disciples those who had similarly forfeited family and property as a result of following Jesus under persecution or occupation. This would have the effect of supporting them and any of their fellows who had similar losses to sustain by extending to them the promises of verses 29-30. Of course, this would require that they too inhabit a world in which eschatological promises had weight and credibility and in which Jesus' authority to promise was an accepted fact.

"Narrative": The capacity of Mark's readers to share this view of reality, on which the story depends for its moral force, would depend in turn upon their familiarity with, and adherence to, the larger story of Jesus. In particular, it would have to include not only his predicted suffering and death, but his remembered resurrection. In other words: for this story of the man who could not follow, and of the disciples who did, to have the effect of asserting the need for sacrifice and forming the capacity to sustain it, the Gospel would have to be read, as it were, back to front. As even Mark's terse introduction (1:1) implies, the community has to know — and believe — the end to make use of the middle.[22]

. . . *and Contemporary Churches'*

For the text to operate for the contemporary church in a fashion analogous to the way it operates within Mark's narrated world, or within the world of the first-century church, certain aspects of the moral world I have

22. Here I am understanding Mark's view of the resurrection and of the Kingdom insofar as it is yet-to-come in a straightforwardly literal way. This is not strictly necessary (although see my note 14, p. 48), and is not the only option taken by other interpreters, who affirm the necessity of attending to the eschatological horizon of the gospel to understand its ethical force. Again, cf. Via, *Ethics of Mark's Gospel*, pp. 7ff.

sketched must continue to have meaning (although not necessarily precisely the *same* meaning). I have argued that the morally central contention of the text is that wealth can prevent its possessors from heeding the call of Jesus (vv. 17-22) or entering the kingdom of God (vv. 23-27). If this is so, then in order actively to be formed by it, modern Christian communities must have *some* notion of an active call of Jesus that might be responded to (or not), and they must continue to have *some* substantive notion of a "kingdom of God" that might be entered (or not). Insofar as these are aspects of a "reality perspective," which draw their content and their credibility from the larger narrative of Jesus and the church, modern Christian communities must have some kind of adherence to the overarching story of the New Testament. These are the most obvious sort of remarks, to be taken at the barest face value.

Bluntly put, there must be some idea that a commitment to Christ might take the form of being called upon to *do* something concrete and distinctive, rather than (for example) simply to believe something, or to live a conventionally decent life. Without the idea of a call to be obeyed, poverty cannot be of *instrumental* value, as wealth cannot serve as a practical obstacle. In the first instance, it does not matter what any particular group sees the Christian mission to be, whether preaching to the unbelieving or healing the sick or disarming nuclear warheads or any number of others; only that it be seen as a pattern of action to which the community, or some number of it, is or could be called. The text can (and does) operate in this way in the present time across a great diversity of circumstances for those who understand their situation as one of sacrifices made for the gospel. What is crucial is the self-understanding of the community.[23]

23. One other possibility exists for a different and very attenuated moral use for this text, a possibility that may well be the most common among North American mainline Protestant churches. This is the use that takes the story as a historical record of a time (now past) when believers were called upon to do something — literally to follow Jesus to Jerusalem, or to risk martyrdom preaching the gospel, or what have you. This would hold up for admiration and gratitude (although not for appropriate emulation) those first-century believers, who were called to risk everything — and did. It might be expected to foster a positive evaluation of the virtues of courage and devotion, but it would not be likely to inspire similar devotion. Indeed, this kind of use could coexist with a tacit or even an explicit rejection of the credibility of all or most of the New Testament narrative, and with the conviction that these (admirable) believers were simply wrong about what they thought was true.

Similarly, it does not matter for this purpose whether the understanding of the kingdom of God be of a future and transcendent reign, or of a present and hidden rule to which allegiance might be given, or of some more complex and dialectical account.[24] It only matters that the idea have *some* content that can elicit and sustain loyalty and desire. Without a concept of a kingdom that can command allegiance, the idea that wealth might compete for that allegiance has no purchase and no weight. In the absence of a shared and vital account of reality that can give content to Mark's eschatological language of kingdom and eternal life, members of modern churches can only listen to this text being read and wonder privately what sort of lunacy might induce anyone to throw away her money (or her life) for — literally — nothing.

At the same time, it is of central importance here that the moral norms or virtues generated by a community's acceptance and appropriation of the Marcan language and thought-world are, in a certain sense, *formal.* This way of understanding the text's moral function can easily accommodate the idea that "great possessions" and "riches" are relative and socially contextual terms, to be defined anew in different settings. It can accommodate a very wide range of accounts of what Christians in particular times and places are called on to do, as well as a variety of theologically distinct understandings of eschatology. Across all these variations, the story can assert and foster the general conviction that possessions can and frequently do remove the liberty essential to responding to the gospel, and that for this reason faithfulness might entail leaving them behind. It can offer a rationale and a context of intelligibility for actual sacrifices. And it can offer support and encouragement to those who have suffered losses in pursuit of ends that are intangible or unrealized, and sustain their courage and their joy in the face of those losses.

24. Although I have tried to indicate briefly why, in view of the prominence of martyrdom as the expected end of faithfulness in Mark's gospel, I think the understanding of Kingdom must have some transcendent or transhistorical "cash value" in order to work in a way analogous to its first-century function as an ethical warrant (see note 14, p. 48).

CHAPTER 4

Luke 12:22-34

Preliminary Questions: Date and Historical Setting

THE CLEAR AUTHORIAL VOICE of the prologues to Luke and Acts, unique among the gospels, plus the famous "we" passages in Acts (e.g., 16:10-17 and 20:5–21:18) have combined to make the question of authorship a focus of unusual attention for this gospel. The traditional association of the two volumes with the "Luke, the beloved physician" of the Pauline letters (Col. 4:14, II Tim. 4:11, Phil. 24) goes back at least to 180 C.E.[1] This hypothesis is still widely, though not unanimously,[2] accepted.

More of a puzzle is precisely how to date Luke's text. On the one hand, Luke's Gospel self-avowedly precedes Acts, which mentions neither the fall of Jerusalem nor events such as the death of James in 62 C.E. or the execution of Paul, thought to have occurred in 66 to 67 C.E. This suggests to some a date in the early 60s.[3] On the other hand, the Gospel uses a version of Mark very like our own, and displays a detailed knowledge of, and interest in, the destruction of the second Temple. Both of these features suggest a date in the later decades of the first century, perhaps 75 to 90 C.E.[4] In any case, all the dates under current consideration place the

1. Cf. esp. Irenaeus, *Adv. Haer.* (iii,i,i; iii, xiv,i).

2. For a good summary of the origin and vicissitudes of the debate on this matter begun by F. C. Baur, see E. E. Ellis, *The Gospel of Luke* (Grand Rapids: Eerdmans, 1974).

3. So E. E. Ellis, *Gospel of Luke.*

4. E.g., W. Kuemmel, *An Introduction to the New Testament* (Nashville: Abingdon Press, 1975), p. 151; J. A. Fitzmyer, *The Gospel According to Luke I–IX* (New York: Doubleday, 1983), pp. 53-57; L. Johnson, *Sharing Possessions* (Philadelphia: Fortress Press, 1981), pp. 2-3.

Gospel's composition in some proximity to the brief but severe Neronian persecutions of the mid-60s, as well as to the Jewish revolt and its brutal suppression.

Something of the audience to which Luke's Gospel is addressed can be inferred from the prologue. It is worded in accordance with accepted literary conventions of the time[5] and dedicated as to a literary patron, thus obviously intended for an audience wider than Luke's own community. At the same time, its concerns with eschatology, the status of Israel, the kingdom of God, and the work of the Holy Spirit mark it clearly as part of the ongoing conversation of the early church, so its purpose cannot be construed as only apologetic or evangelical in the narrow sense. It must be taken to include the instruction and edification of the gentile churches of the "diaspora," scattered throughout Asia Minor, among which Luke had worked. This historical reconstruction, somewhat clearer than that available for Mark's Gospel, provides us with a general context for understanding the world in which Luke wrote and the situation that confronted his first readers.

Although the text we examine in this chapter is discursive rather than immediately narrative, it is not parenetic in the simple sense that, say, a text from the Pauline epistles might be: that is, it is not the author's direct address to his own or other communities. To begin with, he is making use of preexisting accounts (those things that "were delivered" — 1:2), and the variations in style and diction in different parts of the Gospel suggest that he stayed fairly close to his sources much of the time. Moreover, the writer explicitly undertakes to order those sources into a connected narrative, which like all narratives has its own logic and dynamics, creating its own storied world that forms the foreground to which Luke's own world is background. Much of the time the best indication we have of the author's understanding of, and purposes for, the traditions he hands on are the connections he makes between them and the relations into which he places them. Thus we may find the most valuable clues to the moral import of Luke's Gospel in those literary features of structure and context that most clearly reflect his activity as author and redactor.[6]

5. For parallel see Josephus, *Apology,* 1:1-4.

6. This reliance on literary features of the canonical text rather than on historical reconstruction of its sources and setting as a key to interpretation characterizes a number of recent works on Luke/Acts. See on our topic, for example, Luke Johnson's *The Literary*

Very little space need be devoted to establishing the Greek text of this passage, which is exceptionally well attested.[7] Similarly, the text has little syntactical ambiguity or complexity, a fact that is reflected in the general unanimity of its translators. On the whole, the "what" of this passage is rather disconcertingly clear. The translation that follows is once again based on the third edition of the United Bible Societies' Greek New Testament, and differs from several other recent versions only in being slightly more literal.

22 And he said to his disciples: For this reason I tell you, do not worry about your life, what you might eat, nor about your body, what you might put on.
23 For life is more than food, and the body more than the clothing.

24 Think of the ravens, that they neither sow nor reap, they have neither storehouse nor barn, and God feeds them: by how much you surpass the birds!
25 And which of you can, by worrying, add a foot to your height?[8]
26 Therefore, if you cannot do the smallest thing, why do you worry about the other things?

27 Think of the wild lilies, how they grow! They do not toil nor

---

Function of Possessions in Luke-Acts (Missoula: Scholars Press, 1977) and *Sharing Possessions* (Philadelphia: Fortress Press, 1981), as well as his full length commentary, *The Gospel of Luke* (Collegeville, Minn.: Liturgical Press, 1991). More broadly, nonbiblical literary criticism figures in various ways in D. Moessner, *Lord of the Banquet: Literary and Theological Significance of Luke's Travel Narrative* (Philadelphia: Fortress Press, 1989) and C. Talbert's commentary on the overall argument and structure of the gospel, *Reading Luke* (New York: Crossroad, 1982). Robert Tannehill's two-volume work *The Narrative Unity of Luke-Acts* (Philadelphia: Fortress Press, 1986) uses narrative criticism as a cue to understanding the theological stance and purpose of the Lucan corpus.

7. Existing variants are few and not significant: two of them involve the use of the genitive pronoun αὐτοῦ ("his"). Some of the earliest manuscripts omit the pronoun after μαθητὰς (disciples) in v. 22. A large number of manuscripts replace the αὐτοῦ of v. 31 with τοῦ θεοῦ (of God). The third variant concerns an alternate text of v. 27. This gives οὔτε νήθει οὔτε ὑφαίνει ("they neither spin nor weave") instead of οὐ κοπιᾷ οὐδὲ νήθει ("they do not toil or spin").

8. Taking this at face value as a measure of stature; might also be "add a little to your lifespan."

spin; but I tell you, Solomon in all his glory was not arrayed like one of these.

28 But if God thus clothes the grass in a field, which exists today and tomorrow is thrown in an oven, how much more [will he clothe] you, o ones with little faith!

29 And do not look for what you may eat and what you may drink, and do not be anxious;

30 for all the nations of the world pursue these things, and your Father knows that you need them.

31 But rather, look for his kingdom, and these things will be given to you as well.

32 Fear no more, little flock, because it has pleased your Father to give you the kingdom.

33 Sell your possessions and give alms; make for yourselves purses that do not grow old, an unfailing treasure in the heavens where no thief comes near nor moth destroys;

34 For where your treasure is, there too your heart will be.

Paragraphing in the translation is merely to facilitate reading and emphasize rhetorical structure; it reflects no judgments on the sources or history of the canonical text.[9]

Reading the Passage

If there is any consensus about the teachings regarding wealth and possessions that are attributed to Jesus in the Gospels, it is that they are imprac-

9. Scholarly opinion on the appropriate division of this text into literary subunits is divided. There are good and interesting form-critical grounds for a division between vv. 31 and 32, and others argue for a division between 32 and 33. Moreover, these questions intersect with the questions about the text's sources and prehistory, which are unusually complicated because of the complex relation between this chapter as a whole and its parallels in Mark and Luke. These are debated in a wealth of literature speculating about multiple recensions of Q and L and Proto-Luke, which it would be tedious and unhelpful to relate here. Since my interest is in the ethical appropriation of the canonical text, my concern is for thematic unity rather than textual antecedents.

tical. Furthermore, it is agreed, nowhere is the "completely unprudential rigorism of Jesus' ethic"[10] more in evidence than in this passage from Luke's Gospel, which commands us not to seek even the necessities of life, but rather to sell our possessions and give alms. The very extremity of these pronouncements is often taken as evidence of their authenticity.[11] Paradoxically, though, form critics have long agreed that the discourse of chapter 12 belongs in that category of dominical sayings known as "wisdom sayings."[12] These are distinguished for their formal affinities with the Jewish wisdom tradition, which is concerned with the elaboration of principles to which "it is both moral and prudent to conform."[13] Thus there appears to be a wide consensus that the passage at hand contains the impossible admonitions of an idealistic Jesus who understands himself to be giving sound advice! How are we to make sense of this?

It is my contention that the teachings of Jesus related in Luke 12:22-34 are part of an "exhortation to prudence" that shapes Luke's entire chapter, and that they are advanced in light of a self-consistent understanding of reality — a distinctive "reality perspective" — the advocacy of which is central to the moral functioning of the book of Luke. To defend that view, I will, as previously, attend first to the internal movement of verses 22-34, and then to their placement and function within the larger contexts of chapter 12 and of Luke's Gospel as a whole.

Rhetorical Structure of the Passage

Unlike the text from Mark, which at least raises the question of the moral appropriation of a story, this passage leaves little room for doubting its moral force on the face of it. Counting both prohibitions and positive commands, these dozen verses contain fully twelve directives, covering a wide range of mental, emotional, and physical behavior. The language is strong, employing (besides imperatives) exclamatory prefaces (πόσῳ — vv. 24 and 28), repetitions, and formulae such as λέγω δὲ ὑμῖν ("but I tell

10. Reinhold Niebuhr, *Christian Ethics,* p. 23.

11. E.g., generally in R. Bultmann, *Die Geschichte der synoptischen Tradition,* 4th ed. (Goettingen, 1958). Although see remarks on vv. 25 and 32 (pp. 84 and 116).

12. So, e.g., Bultmann, *Synoptischen Tradition,* pp. 102-3; Dalman, *Jesus-Jeshua* (New York: Macmillan, 1929).

13. Verhey, *Great Reversal,* p. 41.

you" — vv. 22, 27) to lend emphasis. It is undeniable that the speaker intends to prompt and to guide action.

Given all this, it is especially interesting that the directives are not given like the Decalogue, as a series of commands or rules, with an assumption of their self-evident force, or with an appeal to divine authority: there is nothing comparable to "for thus says the Lord your God." Instead, the discourse is presented as an *argument*. It commences with διὰ τοῦτο — "for this reason" (a reference to the preceding parable, which will be considered below) and proceeds with admonitions to consider various kinds of evidence. The clauses are linked by logical connectives such as "if . . . then" (v. 26), "for" (vv. 23, 30, 34), and "but" (v. 28). Each of the exhortations functions as the conclusion of an argument providing reasons to recommend that course. Clearly, Jesus is attempting to persuade his hearers, and he does so in the time-honored fashion of the sage who derives principles of prudence and morality from his observation of the world: by appealing to a description of how the world works and relying on his hearers' good sense to recommend the proper course.[14]

14. In fact, the similarities between this teaching (and the Q material generally) and the moral discourses of the Greek philosophers, particularly the Stoic and Cynic teachers who were roughly contemporary, have led some scholars to regard the Jesus of the gospels as more nearly a Hellenistic sage than a Jewish prophet. (See, e.g., F. G. Downing, *Christ and the Cynics* (Sheffield: Sheffield Academic Press, 1988) and B. Mack, *A Myth of Innocence* (Philadelphia: Fortress Press, 1988).

It is undeniable that there are striking parallels both in rhetorical style and in the general treatment of certain topics, including anxiety and possessions. (For a partial list of the closest of such parallels in Luke, see L. Johnson's index of citations from Dio Chrysostom and Epictetus in *The Gospel of Luke*.) However, there are crucial differences as well, differences that go right to the essence of the message in each case.

Briefly: at the heart of the Stoic/Cynic moral tradition is an account of virtue that, following Plato, understands justice as an *inner condition of the soul* characterized by harmony and the proper ordering of all faculties under reason. This virtue, which is immune from direct attack and independent of all social ties, is defined as true happiness. It renders its possessors supremely invulnerable and self-sufficient, and thus indifferent to poverty or even death.

By contrast, the Jewish wisdom tradition appeals to a justice that exists *in the world as it is ordered by a just God.* In the "eschatological wisdom" portrayed in Luke, it is the vindication of God that is hoped for, as it is the judgment of God that is feared. Far from a safety rooted in independence and self-sufficiency, it offers its adherents ultimate safety in a relation of trust and dependence upon God. The treatment of possessions and of anxiety in Luke is merely a corollary of that relationship, an admonition to preserve and rely on it in preference to all else.

Thus Jesus commands his disciples "do not be anxious" and provides three arguments for the inappropriateness of anxiety.[15] It is *inadequate* because it springs from an inadequate understanding of human life (v. 23); it is *unnecessary* because God who feeds the birds will feed them (v. 24); and it is *ineffective* because no one can add anything to his life by it (v. 25). In verses 27-28 Jesus repeats the points of inefficacy (Solomon, for all his greatness, did not secure to himself the beauty of a wildflower) and needlessness ("how much more will he clothe you!"). Verses 29-31 reemphasize the wrongheadedness of concerning oneself with food and drink, this time recommending an alternative goal, presumably based on a right understanding of human life; the disciples are to concern themselves with finding the kingdom of God, and Jesus promises that they will receive the necessities of life as well.

On its own terms, such a solution clearly has everything to recommend it. If God will provide (without our anxiety) what we seek anxiously and with little effect (verse 30) and more and better besides, it is only the part of good sense to accept his gracious gifts, and to be freed of so troublesome a burden. The announcement of blessing that follows immediately suggests that Luke sees Jesus' admonitions in precisely this way: "Fear no more, little flock, for it has pleased your Father to give you the kingdom" (v. 32). But in this blessing, gift and demand are inextricably intertwined. "Fear no more" is a command as well as a comfort, and it is followed by another command that gives flesh to the first: "Sell your possessions and give alms" (v. 33).[16]

Lest there be any doubt about the plain sense of this particular text, the food and drink that the disciples are not to seek is that which is necessary for life (v. 22), and the aorist imperative πωλήσατε ("sell") of verse 33 suggests a single and complete act of divestiture.[17] Significantly

15. This analysis corresponds closely to that offered by I. Howard Marshall for vv. 22-25 in *The Gospel of Luke* (Grand Rapids: Eerdmans, 1978), pp. 526-28. He does not, however, treat the rest of this passage as part of this argumentative structure, nor does he consider the relation of this argument to the broader argument of chapter 12.

16. Talbert in his book recognizes this general structure, and the way in which "Sell your possessions" represents an application or consequence of what has preceded it (*Reading Luke,* pp. 142ff.), but he gives little attention to the force or implications of this directive. He observes, "Although Jesus believed no one can serve God and mammon, he called on his disciples in vv. 33-34 to serve God with money" (p. 143). This seems rather to soft-pedal the text.

17. David Seccombe in his book *Possessions and the Poor in Luke-Acts* (Linz: Studien

though, the reasons advanced here for this act have to do not with the claims of those needing alms, *but with the disciples themselves.* Giving their possessions away constitutes providing themselves with treasure in heaven, where it is safe from earthly contingencies. Moreover, the reason for placing one's treasure in heaven is quite directly stated: "For where your treasure is, there too your heart will be" (v. 34). This is not, of course, a normative statement at all; it is simply a descriptive observation about human beings. It is in fact the foundation of sound advice to anyone wishing to give undivided allegiance to God's kingdom, all perfectly reasonable, *provided* one accepts the description of the world on which it is based. How crucial this provision is, the text itself makes clear.

Luke, who has placed these teachings in the context of a discourse addressed "to his disciples first" (v. 1), emphasizes the particularity of this address in verse 22, with "and he said to his disciples." Jesus deliberately contrasts the behavior he is calling for with that of the "nations of the world" (v. 30), and while the translation of ἔθνή as "unbelievers" is probably too interpretive, it is clear that Jesus means to distinguish the disciples who *know* they have a Father who knows what they need from the nations who must pursue their own survival. If Jesus finds fear and anxiety in his disciples (as is suggested by the present-imperative prohibitions in vv. 22, 29, and 32, and by the present indicative of v. 26) he immediately identifies the root cause as a matter of lack of confidence in God: "O ones with little faith!" (v. 28).

Thus faith is the critical point; what must appear to one without faith as impossible and foolhardy counsel may be seen by those with it to be the only reasonable course, the one based on the truth about human beings and the world in which they live. Faith is absolutely central to the reality perspective on which this passage relies. Just as critical, however, is identifying the object of that faith. It is faith in God's providence, yes, but even more it is faith in Jesus' proclamation of the kingdom as the proper point of orientation for a human life. In Verhey's language, "wisdom is transformed by eschatology."[18] For all its character of prudent counsel,

---

zum Neuen Testament und seiner Umwelt, 1982), assumes that this imperative cannot mean a general divestiture because the text does not include the word *panta* ("all"), and mostly because it seems evident to him that such a directive would be incompatible with the earlier command not to be anxious (pp. 153-54)! Neither of these arguments is very compelling. Contrast R. Tannehill (*Narrative Unity,* pp. 246-48, especially note p. 247), who does take it as a sweeping directive.

18. Verhey, *Great Reversal,* p. 41.

this is not *simply* "enlightened self-interest," a revelation of better means to the same end. There is, after all, a certain edge to an assurance of God's providence based on his care for birds (sold five for two pennies — 12:6) and grass (which tomorrow is thrown into the oven — 12:28)! Of course, the point is that God cares more for his followers than for birds or wildflowers, but the tension remains for all that.[19] Moreover, Luke heightens and underscores this tension by his placement of this passage in the larger context of chapter 12, to which we now turn.

The Structure of Chapter 12: The Prudence of the Kingdom

If one recalls the classical definition of the virtue of prudence as knowledge of what to seek and what to avoid,[20] then Luke 12:1-21 reads like a discourse on the subject. In verses 1-12, admonitions to avoid or "fear" certain things (hypocrisy, v. 1; the condemnation of God, v. 5; blasphemy against the Holy Spirit, v. 10) alternate in a regular pattern with exhortations *not* to fear or be anxious about other things (those who can kill the body, v. 4, testifying before authorities, vv. 11-12). Verse 15 is a warning against greed (πλεονεξία), which is the occasion for the Parable of the Rich Fool, treated below.

Although each admonition has a rationale attached, as in verses 22-34, here the appeals are more directly eschatological, and the disparity between ordinary self-protection and the "prudence" Jesus recommends is unmistakable. Looking at the whole, it is impossible to forget that Jesus delivers this "lecture on prudence" on the road to Jerusalem, after the declaration of 9:22 concerning his own fate. The entire first section deals with the necessity of bearing true witness to Christ, and it presupposes a situation of persecution from which no deliverance is promised. The sparrows are remembered by God (v. 6), not rescued by him, and the Son

19. In emphasizing this duality between confidence in God's providence and the possibility of martyrdom that remains ever in view, I differ from the majority of commentators who understand this passage only as an exhortation to trust in God. While the theme of trust is certainly strong enough, the addition of the arguments about the inadequate conception of life reflected in anxiety, as well as the context, make me think that such a reading is too simple.

20. Aristotle, *Nicomachean Ethics,* VI, 8.

of Man will acknowledge those who acknowledge him, not protect them (v. 8). These exhortations amount to a call to follow Jesus; it is assumed that his followers may well share his end.

In the Parable of the Rich Fool there are two kinds of appeal. One, the common-sense appeal, is acknowledged (at least fitfully) by all, and is expressed in the popular proverb, "you can't take it with you": "this night your soul is required of you, and the things you have prepared, whose will they be?" (v. 20). The other appeal concerns the possibility and obligation of being "rich toward God" (v. 21), and the expectation of being called to account. It must be borne in mind, however, that the rich man who deliberates and chooses his course without regard for *both* his mortality and his accountability is called not evil but a *fool* (ἄφρων — literally "mindless one," v. 20). What unites these disparate appeals here and throughout the chapter, and makes their union intelligible, is Jesus' own "reality perspective."

Just as he is able to recommend "Do not seek what you are to eat or drink" (v. 29) because he sees everywhere the care of the Father who "knows that you need [these things]" (v. 30), so he is able to commend as sober good sense the suicidal-seeming "Do not fear those who can kill the body" because he *knows* the God who has the power (and authority — ἐξουσίαν) "to cast into hell" (v. 5). Both realities are taken with equal seriousness. From this perspective (and from this perspective alone) the behavior Jesus commands *is* prudent. Indeed, it is wisdom itself. Jesus regards human behavior as having ultimate consequences for the actor and her relation with God, consequences no less real for being hidden from immediate view, and so he recommends to his disciples that they act accordingly.

The two parables that immediately follow our passage support this view. They are descriptions of the consequences of contrasting courses of action. The first parable pronounces a blessing on those servants who are awake and prepared to receive their master when he comes (vv. 36-37). The use of the title ὁ υἱὸς τοῦ ἀνθρώπου ("Son of Man" — v. 40) makes explicit the eschatological reference of the passage and the identification of the master with Jesus himself. Yet this parable is an exhortation to readiness that appears to be addressed to those who have already recognized in Jesus' advent the coming of the Master. If they are still being exhorted to readiness (v. 40), in what is that readiness to consist?

Jesus answers Peter's question about the intended objects of this warning with another parable. This time the recipient of the blessing is specified as the "wise and faithful steward" (v. 42), who is found caring well for the household in his charge. He is contrasted with the unfaithful servant, who takes advantage of his master's absence by abusing those under his control and wasting his master's goods in self-indulgence. This servant, Jesus declares, will be severely punished (literally, "cut in two" [!], v. 46) because he "did not make ready, or act according to his (master's) will" (v. 47). The readiness enjoined upon the disciples, then, is the doing of their master's will. It is according to this that the coming of the kingdom is received as blessing or condemnation. Two things are especially noteworthy. One is that the servant's infidelity arises out of his incorrect belief about his master's return; it is his defective understanding of reality that leads to his undoing. The other is that the image of fidelity used by the parable is obedient stewardship of food and drink, suggesting that the area of obedience in question is related to the disposition of material goods.

Thus, the teaching about anxiety and possessions offered in verses 22-34 is placed by Luke between a consideration of appropriate and inappropriate objects of fear (12:1-21) and a vivid parabolic presentation of the blessing or punishment received according to one's readiness for the kingdom (12:35-48) instanced by obedient disposition of goods. In all of these passages, human attitudes and actions are considered as they spring from underlying beliefs, and tend toward certain ends. Acts are considered as attempts to attain certain ends, and critiqued both on grounds of their effectiveness and with regard to the appropriateness of the end they seek. One of the consequences of such a view is the establishment of an extremely close relationship between belief and action.

It has already been observed that adherence to the course recommended by Jesus, in order to be comprehensible, would require acceptance of his proclamation of the kingdom and its priority. By now it should be clear that this acceptance is not to be understood only or chiefly as assent to his claims; rather, it is the ordering of one's life in accord with that priority.[21] Just as *only* those who believe Jesus can be expected to follow his counsel, those who *do* believe *are* expected to follow it. Failure to do so is evidence that those in question do not in fact believe at all; it is

21. For a suggestive statement of this view of the inseparability of action from belief or understanding offered in a different context, see Via, *Ethics of Mark's Gospel,* p. 19.

comparable to affirming one's conviction that a runaway truck is speeding toward one while refusing to move an inch.

Seen in this light, what are traditionally called the "counsels" of Jesus do not have the character of law, and obedience to them is not the *requirement* of faith; it is rather what *follows from* faith, the reasonable response of one who perceives in Jesus the advent of the kingdom and, like Zacchaeus, "receives him joyfully" (19:6). It is difficult to express without sounding circular, but Luke's Gospel affirms that to those who welcome the kingdom, it *is* good news. To one who accepts Jesus' proclamation and is willing to shape her life by it, even the "hard sayings" of chapter 12 are cause for rejoicing; they may be received as a liberation from anxiety, the promise of ultimate security rather than the demand for ultimate risk.[22]

The Theme of Luke's Gospel: Banishing Fear

We have already considered this chapter's repeated exhortations to "fear not" (vv. 4, 7, 32; cf. also vv. 11, 22, 29) in their relation to the warnings that parallel them here as part of an admonition to exercise prudence. The liberating character of Jesus' preaching as presented by Luke is underscored if we also consider them in relation to other settings in Luke where the same formulation occurs.

The phrase "fear not" occurs three times in the first two chapters of Luke, in the birth narratives with which he opens his account (1:13, 1:30, 2:10). Each time it is spoken by an angel to a person frightened by the angel's appearance. But the angel's reassurance is not intended merely to calm the fear associated with any manifestation of divine power. Although that is clearly part of its intent, in each case reasons are offered for confidence and indeed for joy, and they are offered in poetic or hymnic passages that open the sphere of significance to include all of Israel, and finally all the world (1:13-19, 1:30-33, 2:10-12). In this way these passages unite the two Old Testament uses of the formula "fear not": the banishing of fear occasioned by a theophany, and the opening of the liturgical or prophetic salvation oracle.[23] Although the formal parallels with salvation

22. For a similar reading of this text, see Johnson, *Sharing Possessions,* pp. 87-88.

23. Claus Westermann, *Isaiah 40–66* (Philadelphia: Westminster Press, 1969), p. 71.

oracles are limited, the very purpose of these theophanies is the declaration of God's saving act whereby "He has visited and redeemed His people, so that (they), being delivered from the hand of (their) enemies, might serve Him without fear" (1:68, 74). Their purpose is explicitly deliverance from fear.

The puzzling thing about Zechariah's song is that, like the Magnificat, it is a rejoicing in what God *has done,* and it is written using the aorist, as of an action already completed in the past. A great deal of scholarly debate arises over the time references in these passages, which our purposes do not require that we resolve here.[24] One thing seems clear: the freedom from fear, and the rejoicing it brings, have their basis in a conviction of God's salvation so complete as to regard it as already accomplished.

This is also the confidence displayed by Jesus when he says, "It has pleased your Father to give you the kingdom." Although the time referent of the infinitive δοῦναι ("to give") remains open, the decision that has pleased God is rendered in the aorist (εὐδόκησεν), as of a thing already accomplished. Here it is the basis not only of the command "Fear not" but of that other command that is the only concrete directive about property given in the chapter: "Sell your possessions, and give alms" (12:33).

The Moral Use of the Passage: The Implications of Fearlessness

The point to be made here is that Jesus' confidence would free those who shared it from fear and that such freedom would serve as the foundation of a new moral existence. It would create new possibilities of joy as well as of obedience; or rather, the character of such obedience would be joyous itself. This applies to all areas of ethics because it would affect all aspects of moral life, but it has a special relevance to issues of wealth and possessions because possessions are the means used by human beings to extend and protect their lives. But the strength with which they cling to them is

24. See Marshall, *Gospel of Luke,* pp. 83-84 and 90 for a review of the issues concerning the use of the aorist in the cited passages from the infancy narrative, and at 156 and 530 for a discussion of the various possible meanings of the aorist of εὐδοκέω.

only a symptom of their distrust in, and disbelief of, those things that Christ here asserts, and that Christians at least sometimes claim to believe. The problem, from the point of view internal to this passage, *is* a matter of lack of faith. It is the human refusal to accept the good news of the kingdom offered on its own terms that is finally at stake.

This then is the kind of moral significance the text attributes to issues concerning the disposal of possessions. But the evidence of such disbelief cannot be understood as failure to conform to a particular rule about possessions, including the "rule" of complete divestiture proffered in this passage. What has been said about Jesus' commands having more the character of counsels aimed at achieving an end than of laws requiring obedience is borne out by the diversity of the treatment given the question of possessions in the Lucan corpus. Beside the command to sell them all which we find here, Luke unabashedly depicts, commends, and even celebrates a whole range of options from ordinary hospitality (8:2-3, 10:38-42, etc.) to communal ownership (Acts 4:32-37) to the dispersal of half of one's assets (Lk. 19:1-9). The variety of patterns of disposing possessions that are approved in Luke/Acts precludes the formulation of any single material norm as "the" Lucan ethic about ownership.[25] Instead of a rule there is . . . perhaps the best word is an invitation.

In Luke, Jesus offers the kingdom as the only goal worthy of human pursuit. He promises that it will be given (indeed, in a certain sense, is given already) on the single condition that it is sought above all other things. In this passage as well as in the surrounding text, the possibility that so single-hearted a search will risk the disciples' livelihoods and even their lives is implicit. But what is rejected in the rejection of the terms of such a pursuit is not preeminently a moral stance about possessions; it is a comprehensive account of reality that makes it intelligible, even entirely rational, to heed such a call. The paradox of such a summons is that, viewed from the other side, from the assumption of the truthfulness of this account of the world, it is equally a gift. It is "wise counsel," which if followed would enable one to accomplish the ends he desires, to secure his life in fact in the only way it can be secured.

I have argued that the central moral point of the passage from Mark is that possessions can restrict one's liberty to respond to Jesus' call to

25. For a thorough and enlightening discussion, see Johnson, *Sharing Possessions,* pp. 11-29, and also *Possessions in Luke-Acts.*

discipleship, acting as a practical hindrance to hearing and heeding such a call. Here the accent is slightly different. The point of this passage is that what one pursues de facto *is* what one treasures, and in it reposes one's trust and confidence. The trouble with wealth is that, as a putative source of security, it usurps God's role as source and measure and guarantor of life. Luke undertakes to establish as a horizon or possibility for human life a confidence of ultimate blessing so complete as to free people from compulsion about the material needs of their lives.

This confidence partly rests on trust in divine Providence for the provision of ordinary needs: in the language of reference groups established previously, to be a disciple is a matter of belonging to the group of those who know they have a Father in heaven, rather than to the "nations" who must pursue the means of material sustenance. But partly it rests on a different account of security itself, an account that claims that even when they are supplied, material provisions remain continually subject to threat and contingency — to the "moth and rust which corrupt and the thief who breaks in to steal." *Beyond the assurance that God will provide what God's children need, there is the claim that what they need is not finally the things that all pursue, but God's own reign, to which all these are added almost incidentally.*

As before, for its intelligibility this passage requires accepting a distinctive "reality perspective," one that can support the idea that looking for God's kingdom is the only business worth the serious attention of a human being, as well as the only business requiring it. For it to function morally in an analogous way in the modern church, some substantive version of that belief would have to operate. This would have to include confidence in God's capacity and will to provide what was needed by God's people. But beyond that, it would have to include accepting the truthfulness of what Luke offers as an adequate account of human life, one that claims the relation with God as the central need and value of human life. Only such a view could sustain a readiness to incur tangible risks and losses for the sake of securing an intangible but ultimate well-being: a heart undivided in its loyalty to God's reign.

Perhaps the most delicate thing to identify is what exactly is perceived as the "morally important behavior." As serious and flat-footed as is the imperative "Sell your possessions," we have seen that it cannot consistently be taken as Luke's "rule." Instead, it is an invitation to enact and thus to witness to the truth of Luke's proclamation that in Jesus the Dayspring from on high has visited and redeemed his people. By their extraordinary generosity to the poor (21:1-4) or by their voluntary poverty (12:33), by their refusal to call anything their own (Acts 4:32) or by their simple hospitality to the messengers of the kingdom, the disciples celebrate the liberty of the people of God, who live proleptically under God's reign even as they look for the kingdom to come.

But if this did not and does not produce a rule for the Christian treatment of possessions, it does *rule out* certain things; there is no room in this view for business as usual. The ordinary functions of possessions — to ensure status and power and invulnerability over against others — are all excluded. Possessions become useful and acceptable within the Christian community exactly insofar as they become dispensable to their possessors, and thus available for dispersal as the material needs of others, or the spiritual needs of their erstwhile owners, make it expedient. Although it is fair to say that in Luke the disposal of wealth is symbolic or symptomatic rather than being the subject of particular regulations, one does well to remember that symptoms *are* symptoms because they indicate the presence of disease. Only in Luke's Gospel is the blessing of the poor matched by its corresponding denunciation: "Woe to you who are rich, for you have received your consolation!" (6:24).

CHAPTER 5

II Corinthians 8:1-15

Preliminary Questions: Date, Situation, and Literary Integrity

IN MANY RESPECTS, there is an enviable degree of clarity about the historical setting of II Corinthians when compared with the Gospels. We know who wrote it,[1] and where,[2] and we know when it was written to within a very few years (55-57 C.E.).[3] We know the community to which it was written.[4] Between the information provided elsewhere in Paul, the references of Acts, and details provided in the letter itself, we have much more information about what occasioned the composition of this particular chapter than is ordinarily available. We even have Paul's own later

1. With the exception of 6:14–7:1, which some scholars (following Bultmann) hold to be a non-Pauline interpolation, Paul's authorship of II Corinthians is undisputed. See, e.g., G. Bornkamm, "Die Vorgeschichte des sogennanten Zweiten Korintherbriefes," in *Gesammelte Aufsaetze* IV, BEvT 53, pp. 165-70.

2. See II Cor. 2:13 and 7:5.

3. Based on inscriptions dating the proconsulship of Lucius Junius Gallio, before whom Paul appeared, to 51 C.E. This provides an approximate date for Paul's initial visit to Corinth. Allowing time for the sending of I Corinthians and the earlier letter to which it refers in 5:9, and for the "severe letter" to which II Corinthians refers, II Corinthians cannot have been earlier than 55 C.E., or later than about 58 C.E., the latest possible date for Romans, which refers to the collection as already gathered. For a convenient and detailed account of the chronology, see V. P. Furnish's Anchor Bible Commentary *II Corinthians* (New York, Doubleday, 1984).

4. Although H. D. Betz argues that chapter 9 was originally a letter drafted for the Achaian churches generally; see his Hermeneia commentary *2 Corinthians 8 and 9* (Philadelphia: Fortress Press, 1985), pp. 90ff.

report (Rom. 15:26) indicating at least some degree of success for the fund-raising effort.

At the same time, few texts have been the subject of more conjecture or more controversy than II Corinthians as a whole. Further, the importance of this passage in those debates is indicated by the very existence of the commentary of Hans Dieter Betz cited above, which devotes a book-length discussion to only chapters 8 and 9 of the letter. In brief, the controversy concerns the status of the text we have as II Corinthians, and the boundaries and the relation of several subsections of the text. Most (though not all)[5] scholars agree that these were not originally part of a single letter. Proposals for the number of fragments range from two to five. The case for regarding canonical II Corinthians as a composite document is strengthened by the lack of clear external attestation or reference to the letter prior to Marcion's canon in the mid-second century.[6]

Our passage is important in these debates because of the abrupt change of topic that marks the beginning of chapter 8, and because of the peculiar opening of chapter 9 ("You have no need for me to write to you concerning the collection for the saints"), which strikes many readers as an unlikely follow-up on the preceding discussion. These features have suggested to some scholars that chapters 8 and 9 (individually or jointly) form all or part of another letter or letters from Paul to Corinth, or to the cities of Achaia more generally. Other "seams" in the text have been thought to be visible at 6:14 to 7:1 (see my note 1, p. 73), and between chapters 10 to 13 and the preceding body of the text.

Inseparable from these questions, and from the literary analyses that occasion them, are the various efforts at historical reconstruction that seek to untangle the course of events that took place at Corinth between Paul and his recalcitrant congregation. In part, these efforts are motivated by historical curiosity about the character and career of the apostle Paul and his relations with the congregations he founded. Equally they are occasioned by the effort to understand the thought of Paul as it appears in this letter, in many ways the most personal and the most difficult of all his surviving correspondence.

5. E.g., Frances Young and David Ford offer an interesting case for the unity of the letter in their book *Meaning and Truth in II Corinthians* (Cambridge: Cambridge University Press, 1987), pp. 27-57, which is discussed below, p. 79.

6. Though some find allusions or paraphrases in the letters of Ignatius. See A. Barnett, *Paul Becomes a Literary Influence* (Chicago: University of Chicago Press, 1941), pp. 152-70, 203-7.

There appear to be nearly as many theories about the correct partitioning of II Corinthians as there are commentators on the text, and a corresponding diversity of accounts of the nature and the chronology of Paul's difficulties with the Corinthian congregation(s). A review of these hypotheses and the arguments marshalled for them is beyond the scope of the present inquiry, and in any case a comprehensive and detailed account is readily available in Betz's commentary.[7] Critics of the partition theories, on the other hand, point to the complete absence of any manuscript evidence for the alleged composite character of the letter.[8]

Our interest in these matters is confined to what is needed to understand the shape and the import of Paul's appeal in 8:1-15 of the letter. In the absence of any resolution to the textual and historical questions surrounding II Corinthians, we cannot rely on its present placement within the letter for clues to its meaning or its moral force. Instead we must attempt to understand the reasoning internal to this chapter in its own right and in its relation to the themes of the Corinthian correspondence and Paul's theology more generally.

Since we are dealing here for the first time with direct exhortation to an identified community (as opposed, e.g., to teaching embedded in a narrative or with the transmission of a preexisting tradition), it will be helpful to review briefly what we do know of the situation Paul was addressing. He was writing from Macedonia, a predominantly rural and agricultural area suffering from poverty and depopulation,[9] to the Christians in Corinth, an ancient city that had seen a return of economic activity and prosperity since the days of its razing (146 B.C.E.) and refounding (44 B.C.E.) by Rome. He is in the latter stages of a campaign to gather funds from the Gentile churches for the Christian community in Jerusalem, a campaign that he had begun at least a year previous to this writing. (See Gal. 2:10, I Cor. 16:1-4, and later Rom. 15:25-27, 30-31, as well as Acts 11:29-30, 24:17.)

Scholars have conjectured about Paul's possible motives for agreeing to take up this collection. Of course there is the expressed desire to provide

7. *2 Corinthians,* pp. 3-36.

8. E.g., A. Stephenson, "A Defense of the Literary Integrity of II Corinthians" in *The Authorship and Integrity of the New Testament* (London: S.P.C.K., 1965); W. Kuemmel, *Introduction to New Testament.*

9. Betz, *2 Corinthians,* pp. 50ff.

relief and support for the Jerusalem church. In addition, Romans 15:30-31 suggests that Paul is particularly eager to demonstrate his goodwill to the community in Jerusalem in view of the history of tension and misunderstanding between Paul and its leaders. The collection also represents tangible evidence of the unity of the church across the boundaries of Jew and Gentile, a major theme in Paul's theology. Some have seen additional motives in the "missionary theology" of Romans 11, and in the fulfillment of Old Testament prophecies about the eschatological pilgrimage of the Gentiles,[10] but these are more speculative, and are not reflected anywhere in Paul's own discussion.

There has also been speculation about the background and extent of the economic distress experienced within the Jerusalem congregation. Some think the difficulty may be the result of economic boycotting aimed at Christians specifically, while others suppose it is the result of the liquidation of assets mentioned in Acts 2. Yet a third group attributes the hardship to more widespread and general economic conditions. The truth is that we do not have enough information to make any judgment with confidence, and our purpose of understanding Paul's moral argument does not require one.

Text, Translation, and Literary Genre

Despite the controversies about the unity of the text of II Corinthians as a whole, the manuscript tradition is unanimous and well attested, and there is only one textual variant of any significance in our passage.[11] Syntactical ambiguity is also minimal, although sentence structure is sometimes complex or awkward, and several key words carry a number of possible meanings among which translators must choose. Variations in translation are due to these features of the text and to efforts to render the tone and nuance of the language in English.

My aim in the translation that follows is to reflect as clearly as possible

10. J. Munck, *Paul and the Salvation of Mankind,* English edition tr. F. Clarke (Richmond: Knox Press, 1959). See also D. Georgi, *Die Geschichte der Kollekte des Paulus fuer Jerusalem* (Hamburg: Reich, 1965).

11. This is in v. 7, where the reading ἡμῶν εν ὑμῖν ("[from] you to us") is very doubtful. The other major possibility is ὑμῶν ἐν ἡμῖν ("from us to you"). See my note 19, p. 78.

Paul's consistent use of certain words that are important for two reasons. First, the repetition of single words used in a variety of senses (e.g., χάρις in vv. 1, 4, 6, 7, and 9) establishes connections or echoes that are often not apparent in the English translation. In addition, many of these terms have broader theological meanings and associations in Paul's writing as well as the more restricted or technical uses that may be employed here, associations that are sometimes germane to interpretation. Where different words must be used in the translation of terms that are the same in Greek, this will be indicated in the accompanying notes. With the exception noted in verse 7, the translation is once again based upon the United Bible Societies Greek text of the New Testament.

1 We make known to you, brothers and sisters, the grace of God which has been given in the churches of Macedonia:
2 that in the midst of a great trial[12] of suffering, the fullness[13] of their joy and the depth of their poverty overflowed[14] into the wealth of their openheartedness;[15]
3 that [they gave] according to their ability, I testify, and beyond their ability, of their own choice,
4 fervently begging of us the favor[16] of sharing in the ministry[17] to the saints,
5 and not just as we hoped, but first gave themselves to the Lord and to us by God's will.
6 As a result, we have asked Titus so that, as he had already begun, so also he should complete this [act of] grace among you.

12. δοκιμή — the word means a test or proof, and is used by Paul most often in the sense of a test of faith, where the outcome is positive. It is the same word as that used in v. 8, of the proof of love that will be provided by the Corinthians' contribution.

13. περισσεία.

14. περισσεύω, verb form of περισσεία from v. 2.

15. ἁπλότητος, most commonly "simplicity" or "guilelessness": in monetary contexts it is often translated "generosity," but it speaks rather to attitude and motive in giving than to the amount of the gift.

16. χαρίς again, the same word translated "grace" in vv. 1, 6, 7, and 9.

17. διακονία means simply service (as "deacon" means server), in other contexts connoting service at table. It is used in Paul and Acts of the practical services such as food distribution and of those who performed them. It is translated variously "ministry," "relief," "benevolence," etc.

7 But as in every way you are full[18] — of faith and of speech and of knowledge and of all diligence and of love toward us[19] — see that you are full also of this grace.

8 I say this not as a command, but as using the diligence of others to try[20] the genuineness of your love as well.

9 For you know the grace of our Lord Jesus Christ, that for your sake he being rich became poor, in order that by his poverty you might become rich.

10 And I give you an opinion in this: for it is best for you, who last year began not only to do this but to desire it, [11] now to complete what you began, so that your eagerness in desiring it may be matched by your finishing it out of what you have.

12 For if the eagerness is there, it is acceptable according to what one has, not what one has not.

13 Not that there should be ease to others and suffering to you, but that out of equality[21] [14] your present fullness should supply their lack, in order that their fullness may supply your lack, so that there may be equality.[22]

15 As it is written: "The one [who gathered] much had no excess, and the one [who gathered] little had no lack."

Although this passage (along with 9:6-15) represents Paul's most extended discussion on the topic of the economic obligations of Christian communities to one another, it does not have many of the features of moral exhortation. It is primarily persuasive rather than didactic or hortatory in tone. Moreover, it seems to be curiously indirect in its approach when compared with Paul's discussions of other moral issues. The opening citation of the behavior of the Macedonian churches strikes many readers as odd or even as an embarrassment, as if Paul is trying to elicit a large

18. περισσεύω — same verb as in v. 2.

19. Adopting here, against the narrow decision of the UBS text committee, the ὑμῶν ἐν ἡμῖν reading as more intelligible in context and equally well attested.

20. δοκιμάζω — verb form of noun translated "trial" in v. 1.

21. ἰσότητος (nom. ἰσότης) — most commonly "equality," may also be translated "equity" or "fairness," as in Colossians 4:1. See my note 40, p. 87, on interpretation.

22. ἰσότης — see note 21.

contribution by making the Corinthians either competitive or ashamed of their relative performance.[23]

An important strand of interpretation has taken this use of the "encomium," a standard technique of Greco-Roman oratory, as a clue to understanding the genre to which the letter belongs. These commentators have found in this chapter (and the following) several rhetorical techniques and characteristics that are common to commercial and bureaucratic letters preserved from the Greco-Roman period. Thus Betz[24] (following Windisch)[25] finds formal and structural parallels to correspondence between business or government officials authorizing envoys for various tasks. Betz finds common features of vocabulary and syntax and the use of similar rhetorical devices, and takes these similarities as a key to interpretation. He calls these two chapters (which he sees as addressed originally to different communities) "administrative or business letters" and finds them "distinctly bureaucratic in tone."[26]

Frederick Danker[27] follows Betz's lead in interpreting Paul's letter in light of the forms of Greco-Roman letter writing. He likens it to several texts in the literature of the period in which the public beneficence of philanthropists or government officials is praised, and further contributions solicited.

The very interesting book by Young and Ford[28] uses the same kind of rhetorical analysis to reach a very different conclusion. They argue that II Corinthians is a unified apologetic epistle, conforming to that genre in its structure and in the use of deliberately contrasting tones from sympathetic persuasion to outright confrontation. In their view, these conventions of Greco-Roman apologetics account for the shifts in tone that have led to the various partition theories.

23. So, e.g., Ernest Best, in his *Interpretation* commentary (Atlanta: John Knox Press, 1987), pp. 75-76, 84.

24. Ibid., pp. 129ff.

25. W. Windisch, *Der Zweite Korintherbrief* (Goettingen: Vandenhoeck & Ruprecht, 1924).

26. Ibid., p. 134.

27. (ACNT) *II Corinthians* (Minneapolis: Augsburg Publishing House, 1989), pp. 20-25, 116-24. See also his *Benefactor: Epigraphic Study of a Greco-Roman and New Testament Semantic Field* (St. Louis: Clayton Publishing House, 1982).

28. Frances Young and David Ford, *Meaning and Truth in II Corinthians* (Cambridge: Cambridge University Press, 1987), pp. 27-57.

However these epistolary conventions may be affecting the structure and style of the chapter,[29] and even influencing its vocabulary, I think it crucial to attend to the way in which Paul transforms any genre even as he borrows from it and to the distinctive meaning given to words by Paul's own usage.[30] There is, for example, a marked contrast between the instances cited by Danker, which praise the "grace" of various wealthy patrons and emperors in language likening them to gods,[31] and the rhetoric of II Corinthians. Paul calls even the impoverished Macedonians' extraordinarily generous gifts not "Godlike" but God's own, and understands them as manifestations of God's grace, which precedes, occasions, motivates, and makes them possible.[32] So strong is the emphasis upon the priority of the divine χάρις to any human gift or favor that Paul seems almost to satirize the rhetoric of benefaction that he is thought to have appropriated. To explicate and defend this point of view, I turn to an analysis of the chapter.

Reading Paul's Appeal

Verses 1-5

Paul's opening statement is a report on the "grace of God" (χάριν τοῦ θεοῦ — v. 1), which has been given to the churches of Macedonia. This grace is manifest first in their joy even in the midst of "a great trial of suffering" (v. 2), a theme touched upon several times elsewhere in the letter (e.g., 1:5, 6:3-10, 7:4). It is this fullness of joy that, together with the depth of their poverty, has "overflowed into the openheartedness" (ἁπλότητος — "simplicity" or "generosity" — v. 2) that Paul calls wealth.

29. Although I find the elaborate rhetorical strategies attributed to Paul by Betz unlikely, as even Danker hints (*II Corinthians,* p. 24).

30. This implicit criticism of the rhetorical analysis of Betz and Danker does not apply to the work of Young and Ford *(Meaning and Truth).* Their analysis is very sensitive to the distinctive use to which Paul puts this structure.

31. *II Corinthians,* pp. 20-24.

32. So Bultmann: "Chapters 8 and 9 may not be interpreted from a humanistic ideal of character (nobility), but rather from Paul's view of the collection as a χάρις in which he and the communities may cooperate" (in his brief but suggestive exposition in *The Second Letter to the Corinthians* [Minneapolis: Augsburg Publishing, 1985], p. 253).

It is peculiar to think of deep poverty overflowing into wealth, but here the riches are emphatically not the gifts of the Macedonians, however substantial they may have been. They are the divine gifts of joy and single-hearted generosity. It is precisely the fact that the Macedonians give out of poverty and not out of wealth that makes their gift a manifestation or sign of God's grace, and so in a sense their poverty is the proof of having received the "wealth" of God. Thus Paul describes their giving as παρὰ δύναμιν (literally "beyond [their] power" — v. 3), suggesting that only God's power makes such a gift possible.

The connection between the act of giving and God's own grace is underscored in verse 4 by the reuse of the word χάρις as a designation for the Macedonians' joining in the collection, as well as by the constellation of meanings attached to the other key terms in the sentence.[33] They beg of Paul the "grace" of "sharing" (κοινωνίαν — means as well "community," "fellowship," and "participation") in the "ministry" to the saints (διακονίας — meaning literally service, this is the root of "deacon" as well as of Paul's word for himself as "minister" of the gospel). In a way impossible to express in English with similar economy, Paul interweaves the concepts of gift, grace, favor, and blessing to present the very act of giving as itself a gift of God, a means of participation through service in the fellowship of the saints, which is also God's blessing.[34]

Verse 5 finishes the description of the Macedonians' participation in a way consonant with the use of ἁπλότητος (translated "openheartedness") in verse 2. Paul says of them that their giving was "of their own choice" and was the expression of their self-dedication to God through Paul, thus devoid of other motives and free of constraint: a "guileless generosity" indeed.

Verses 6-9

The phrase εἰς τὸ (translated "as a result" — v. 6) suggests that it is Paul's rejoicing in this triumph of grace and graciousness that leads him to send

33. A short and useful discussion of the variety of uses and meanings of χάρις in this passage is provided in Ford and Young, *Meaning and Truth,* pp. 96-98.

34. This is one of the many places that justify Nils Dahl's observation that in II Corinthians 8 and 9, "[Paul] expresses himself in a way which is impossible to translate." *Studies in Paul* (Minneapolis: Augsburg Publishing House, 1977), p. 31.

Titus to Corinth, "in order that . . . he might complete this grace [χάρις again] among you." "Grace" here is usually taken in its sense of "gift" to refer to the collection that is to be finished, but it might be taken to refer as well to the character of graciousness that is to be perfected in the Corinthians themselves.

This verse confirms what we know from the reference in I Corinthians 16:1-4, that the Corinthians had already been apprised of the collection for the Jerusalem church, perhaps by Titus on a previous visit, and had agreed to take part in it. This prior agreement sets the stage for the single piece of direct exhortation Paul offers in this passage: praising the Corinthians as full of all gifts, he concludes, "see that you are full of this grace as well" (v. 7).[35] But immediately he disclaims a desire to command their obedience: instead they are to understand him as conducting a trial (δοκιμάζω — verb form of "trial" in v. 2), using the generosity of the Macedonians to prove what Paul (rhetorically at least)[36] assumes to be the genuineness of the Corinthians' love that he has just praised (v. 8).

But he cannot leave it at that, for it is not the churches of Macedonia that can provide the ultimate example of generosity. For Paul, the motive and the very meaning of grace are given by God's own grace, uniquely and preeminently in Christ, and so he reminds them in a single sentence so compact and so perfectly balanced that many have thought it must be liturgical in origin: "For you know the grace of Christ, that for your sake he being rich became poor, in order that by his poverty you might become rich" (v. 9). It is *because* (γαρ — v. 9) they know the story that Paul here renders so tightly in economic terms, because they know themselves to be the beneficiaries of God's gracious generosity, that the Corinthians can be exhorted "be full of this grace as well."

35. This takes the ἵνα clause of v. 7 as imperatival; cf. C. F. D. Moule, *An Idiom Book of the Greek New Testament* (New York: Cambridge University Press, 1959), p. 144.

36. Many commentators draw attention to the parallel between the commendations of v. 7 and the opening "congratulations" of I Cor. 1:5-7 (e.g., Danker, *II Corinthians,* p. 124, and A. Barnett, *Paul Becomes a Literary Influence* [Chicago: University of Chicago Press, 1941], p. 222), but none of them mention the strong possibility that the latter must be taken somewhat ironically in view of the stinging rebukes that follow it (cf. I Cor. 4:7-8). If the present text is at least partly ironic (and it is difficult to see how it could fail to be in view of what we know of Paul's difficulties with this congregation), then Paul has rather deftly used praise to lay a claim on better conduct than he might otherwise expect from the Corinthians.

Verses 10-15

It is not enough, however, that the Corinthians yield their money for the collection. Paul says of them that they began the collection "last year," and in an awkward-seeming phrase, declares that they were "eager [literally "beforehand"] not only in the doing but in the desiring" (v. 10). The point Paul stresses by this inversion is that they not only did what was required but were quick to *desire* to do it; it is this ready desire to help that is to be matched by the fulfillment of the commitment (v. 11). But the doing cannot be divorced from the desire; according to verse 12, it is this attitude of willingness that makes any gift that corresponds to one's resources acceptable. As implied by the designation of generosity as ἁπλότητος in verse 2, it is not merely the quantity of the gift but the single-heartedness of its giver that qualifies it as a sign of, and response to, God's own gift.

In verses 13-14 Paul offers a principle that is to govern the Corinthians' response to the needs of Jerusalem. In contrast to the ultimate grace of Christ, which exchanges wealth for poverty, Paul tells them that they are not required to give ease to others at the cost of suffering to themselves. The aim is to be equality in the meeting of needs within the community, with the surplus of one providing for the deficiency of another, and reciprocity (in principle if not in fact) is assumed. With the quotation from Exodus 16:18 (v. 15) Paul alludes to the miracle of the manna, in which God's provision for his people was an exact sufficiency, which could only be distributed according to need, and not hoarded for an uncertain future. This equality is now to be duplicated among them, not by miraculous intervention, but by the joy and gratitude of God's people "overflowing into the wealth of single-hearted generosity" (v. 2).

Thus the passage ends as it began, with the theme of God's grace, which is the source of joy in affliction and generosity in poverty, as it was the source of food in the wasteland. The reality of God's grace can be verified, as its gifts have a character that can be tried and proven. Its joy endures through suffering, its generosity is without guile (vv. 1-2), and the love it bestows demonstrates itself in acts (v. 8). Therefore the community formed by that grace is one marked by openheartedness and equity, in which gifts are given without mixed motives, resources are shared, and the needs of all are met — and its norm is equality.

The "Economy" of Grace: II Corinthians 8:1-15 in Context

Despite the debate over the original unity of the text we have as II Corinthians, it is still necessary and appropriate to look at this passage as it relates to the themes of the rest of the epistle. Whatever the particulars of the boundaries and chronological sequence of alleged fragments within the canonical text, there is no dispute that the whole was written to a single group over a period of (at most) a year or two. Although the textual difficulties preclude any appeal to the details of organization and structure as keys to interpretation, the consistent use of certain words and motifs throughout the letter testifies to the integral connection in Paul's thought between his appeal for funds for Jerusalem and his broader theological concerns.

I have spoken above of Paul's rendering of the gospel in terms of an economic metaphor in 8:9; while this is the preeminent example of such a metaphor, it is not by any means the only one in the epistle. The Holy Spirit is twice called an ἀρραβῶν (1:22, 5:5) of salvation. Often translated as "an earnest" or "a guarantee," the word literally means "a down payment" or "deposit."[37] Similarly, the gospel that Paul preaches is a "treasure" (θησαυρὸν — 4:7), and his defense of his ministry includes the claim that though "treated as poor . . . [he makes] many rich," and "having nothing, [he] possesses everything" (6:10). Although Paul repeatedly refers to himself as poor (as he has referred to the Macedonian church in 8:2), it is always in immediate conjunction with the wealth of God's grace or gift in Christ, which "abounds" and is said to "overflow" in encouragement, joy, and thanksgiving (1:5, 4:15, 7:4, 8:2, etc.). All in all, the word περισσεύω (abound) and its variants occurs twelve times in chapters 1 through 9. Despite the continuing theme of poverty and affliction (1:4-10, 4:7-12, 6:4-10, 8:2, 11:24-28), the impression conveyed is one of fullness and sufficiency, indeed of super-abundance. Out of the inexhaustible resources of God, Paul and his converts are comforted (1:5-7), led (2:14), transformed (3:18), enlightened (4:3-6), empowered (12:9), and veritably overcome with grace, which grace naturally overflows from them onto one another, whence it is returned to God as joy and thanksgiving (1:11, 4:15, 8:2). Nor is this sense of abundance finally compromised by the "poverty"

37. Bauer, Arndt, Gingrich, and Danker, *Greek-English Lexicon,* p. 109.

of which Paul speaks, for in this peculiar economy, treasure comes "in earthen vessels" (4:7) only to make clear that its source is God, whose "power is made perfect in weakness" (12:9).

The implications of this economy for the collection for Jerusalem are made explicit in chapter 9 of the letter. Here Paul promises that God "is able to cause all grace to abound toward you . . . *so that* always having all self-sufficiency in every thing you may abound in every good work" (9:8). God will further "increase the fruit of your righteousness" (v. 10), and "enrich you for all generosity" that not only supplies the needs of the saints but "overflows in many thanksgivings to God" (v. 12). In verse 13, Paul makes it clear that every aspect of this ministry — the projected faith and obedience of the Corinthians, their generosity toward the Jerusalem church, the resources that meet the needs of the church, and the prayerful gratitude of the recipients — is the gift and glory of God (v. 13). It is evidence of "the surpassing grace of God" (v. 14) in which Paul exults in 9:15: "Thanks be to God for His inexpressible gift!"

The Moral Use of the Text

Structure of the Moral Appeal: Generosity as Gift and Imitation

Perhaps the central thing to note about the moral appeal of this text is what a modern commentator would call its "theocentrism." It is God's grace to the Macedonian churches that is praised, rather than the behavior of the churches themselves (v. 1). Even the exhortation to the Corinthians is not "be benevolent" or "be charitable," as of a character that might reside in them, but "be filled with this *gift* [presumably from God] as well" (v. 7); we have already seen that the foundation of this call is Christ's own generosity in exchanging his wealth for their poverty. Christ is the measure of grace, providing both the model for their imitation and the liberty that makes imitation possible. Clearly Paul regards God as the original and preeminent Giver.

Likewise, he provides scant opportunity to enjoy the pride and superiority conferred in ancient times as in modern by the status of donor.[38] Paul

38. Contrast the discussion of Danker, *II Corinthians,* pp. 20ff. and 116-28.

treats the material inequality that occasions this appeal as a temporary undesirable circumstance, one that is in the natural course of things entirely reversible (v. 14), and one whose effects are to be minimized as a matter of policy. There is no occasion to identify with contrasting "reference groups" like "we the rich versus you the poor," or "we the benevolent versus you the improvident"; there is only the one "we," which includes Macedonians and Corinthians and Christians in Jerusalem, all of those who have been enriched by the grace and gifts of Christ. Ford and Young offer an apt summary:

> What seems to have happened is that the inexhaustible generosity of God places everyone in the position of his clients and therefore owing him thanks; but among the clients themselves there is no basis for anything other than equality or uncalculating generosity, and so all patron-client relationships are relativized.[39]

Also noteworthy is the near absence of any reference to the actual neediness of the Jerusalem church. This passage makes no appeal to the natural sympathies of the Corinthians that might be aroused by a depiction of the sufferings of Jerusalem, which are alluded to only once and then obliquely (v. 13). The only real emotional appeal is to the generosity of Christ, who exchanged his wealth for their poverty, which is used to invite the Corinthians to "prove" the genuineness of their love.

The effect of this tight focus on God as the originator of all gifts, including generosity, and on the extraordinary debt in which the Corinthians (together with all believers) stand, is to reinforce Paul's emphasis on the singleness of motive that characterizes giving that is the fruit of God's grace. In fact, it is the willing and disinterested nature of the gift that constitutes the behavior that is perceived as having moral significance. Therefore, everything about the appeal is designed to prompt a responsive generosity without inflating the Corinthians' sense of power or self-importance.

But the fact that the character rather than the amount of the gift is crucial does not mean that the passage provides no instruction as to what constitutes an appropriate material response to needs within the Christian community. On the one hand, Paul indicates that he hoped for a response

39. *Meaning and Truth,* p. 179. For a full and provocative discussion of "God's economy" in II Corinthians, see ibid., pp. 166-204, to which my treatment is indebted.

"according to [their] ability" from the Macedonians (vv. 3-5), and he twice assures the Corinthians that they need only give "according to what they have" (vv. 11-12). On the other hand, they are to give ἐξ ἰσότητος ("out of [a desire for] equality") and ὅπως γένηται ἰσότης ("in order that there may be equality").[40] Both the motive and the aim of sharing resources is to be that the needs of all be equally addressed. Moreover, the story Paul chooses for illustration, in which each Israelite in the wilderness receives the amount of food needed for that day regardless of what is collected, suggests that he proposes this as a serious standard for giving. Interestingly, Paul makes no case for this standard; he rather assumes that equality in the meeting of needs is the natural goal in the economic relations of the Christian communities. It is the material expression of the unity of all those, "Jew or Greek, slave or free, male or female," who are made one in Jesus Christ.

The Implications of Equality

It is difficult to imagine how such an assumption — so radical in the present situation of enormous disparities in wealth between Christian communities — could function in the contemporary church without being literally revolutionary. It could be objected that with Christian congregations so much larger and more widespread in the modern world, the logistical and administrative difficulties alone preclude any economic sharing on this analogy. But even if the sphere of such sharing were restricted geographically to churches within a single locale, the effect of trying to achieve equality in the meeting of needs would be incalculable. At the very least, the use of personal funds would have to be justified in terms of the needs of the nearest Christian neighbors, and no limitation on sharing short of equality could be assumed.

The result need not take the form of anything so fixed or rigid as a rule. In fact, a rule requiring equal distribution of assets is excluded on the one hand by Paul's proviso about the necessity of an attitude of

40. As noted previously, ἰσότης may be translated "equity" or even "fairness" as well. Either of these translations will suffice, so long as it is understood that in this context the idea includes a normative pressure toward equality in the response to need; it is not a mere procedural fairness corresponding to what we call "equal opportunity."

willingness to qualify a gift as a χάρις (8:12, and see 9:5-7), and on the other by the controlling example of Christ, who exchanges his wealth for poverty on behalf of the church (v. 9). From the standpoint of Paul's carefully couched appeal, such an enforced parity would be at the same time too much and too little. But taking Paul's principle with any seriousness *would* create a normative pressure toward equality, at least until real needs within the wider Christian community could be met.

The striking thing about such a thought experiment is that this norm (unlike those proffered in our passages from Mark and Luke) requires no explicit eschatological underpinnings. There is no direct appeal to a transcendent kingdom of God, or to a coming judgment. Instead, the case rests entirely on Paul's readers understanding themselves as having a share in the narrative that Paul presupposes when he says "For you know the grace of Christ, that for your sake he became poor . . ." (v. 9). This shared story creates the single reference group, the relevant "we" who witness to and manifest the gift of God's grace in their grace toward one another. Of course, it is crucial that this text is addressed to the church, which is always for Paul the community that looks not only backward to the redemption Christ has accomplished but forward to its full realization in the world. Part of the vocation and identity of the church, the point and purpose of its collective life, is to show forth the character of that awaited redemption, including the creation of God's one people out of "Jew and Greek, male and female, slave and free." While the grace-filled life of the church is rooted in the history of what Christ has done, it also points forward to the revelation of what Christ will yet do.

The other point of contrast between this and the Gospel passages already addressed is the direction (so to speak) of the moral pull that is being exerted. The Gospel texts hold a vertical tension between the world's goods and one's liberty for and loyalty to God's kingdom, and the central concern is with the divine-human relationship. Here a horizontal tension exists between concern for one's own needs and the needs of sisters and brothers who are for the most part unknown, and the central concern is human relationship between believers. This is emphatically not to say that this is an "ethical" as opposed to a "religious" norm. Within the world of Paul's thought such a distinction is unintelligible, and both the motive and the capacity for generosity rest entirely upon the prior generosity of Jesus Christ. But here the gift of liberty from false loyalties and from anxiety that is given by faith in Christ overflows into the community in the form of generosity, and returns as gratitude. God's gift becomes an invitation to enter into the fellowship of those who share a common abundance of grace, and thus find reason and capacity for generosity even in the midst of want.

This is a place where the moral implications of being a part of a community formed by the story of Jesus Christ are made clear and concrete. Accordingly, the capacity of this text to contribute to the moral formation and guidance of contemporary congregations depends on the character of their allegiance to the story they routinely affirm when they recite the creeds. Expressly, it depends on their experiencing themselves as the objects of God's generosity, gifted and graced in Jesus Christ, and thus "enriched for every good work."

CHAPTER 6

James 5:1-6

Preliminary Questions: Authorship, Date, Venue, and Situation

ALMOST EVERYTHING about the historical background of this epistle has been disputed. Attributed to James the Just[1] by Origen in 253, the letter lacks earlier outside attestation and appears to have been unknown in the West until much later. It was not recognized as canonical in the West until the late fourth century (the Synod of Hippo, 393 C.E.), suggesting either late composition or a very limited circulation prior to the fourth century. This lack of external evidence, plus the polemical use of Pauline language about justification by faith, have caused many to disregard Origen's ascription as requiring a date improbably early.[2]

Also problematic for the traditional view is the idiomatic and literary quality of the Greek of the letter. It has seemed improbable to many that the son of a Jewish carpenter from Galilee would have had sufficient education and sufficient exposure to Greek culture to write such a document. Accordingly, scholars have developed alternative theories about authorship, such as that attributing the letter to a later Gentile God-fearer converted to Christianity and writing pseudonymously.[3] With these

1. Traditional designation for Jesus' brother, leader in Jerusalem from approximately 40-62 C.E.

2. So for example, W. Kuemmel, *Introduction to New Testament;* W. Schrage, "Der Jakobsbrief" in *Die Katholischen Briefe,* NTD 10 (Goettingen, 1973); J. Cantinat, (SB) *Les Epitres de S. Jacques et de S. Jude* (Paris, 1973); and S. Laws, (HNTC) *A Commentary on the Epistle of James* (New York: Harper and Row, 1980).

3. See S. Laws, *A Commentary on the Epistle of St. James* (New York: Harper and Row, 1980), pp. 36-42.

various theories about authorship go hypotheses about the geographical location of its composition, which have placed the writer everywhere from Egypt[4] (based on the relative abundance of text fragments in that area) to Rome[5] (on the theory, not widely held, that the Shepherd of Hermas reveals some degree of literary dependence on James).

But the association of the letter with James the Just and with Palestine is defended by some scholars as well. Some of these date the letter during his tenure in Jerusalem, arguing that the lack of actual contact between the view James refutes and the real position of Paul is evidence for a date before the circulation of Paul's letters rather than after.[6] Others think the letter is composed of Jacobean material (either oral or written) compiled at a later date, either by James himself at the end of his life or by some Greek editor soon afterward.[7]

It is not possible to take a definitive position on most of the historical questions of date, authorship, and venue I have noted. Naturally, some arguments seem more persuasive than others. On the whole, I am inclined to regard the letter as addressed to Jewish Christians by a Jewish Christian from Palestine in the mid-to-late first century. However, the ambiguities outweigh the evidence, and a clear conclusion seems unlikely to come any time soon.

Tied up with the unanswered questions about the date and geographical provenance of the epistle are questions about the situation that it assumes and is intended to address. Everyone agrees that the generality of address (1:1) precludes reading details of the recipients' situation from the references of the epistle. Interpreters who regard the epistle as essentially a compilation of traditional material[8] further argue that nothing of the writer's situation may be inferred; he is simply transmitting inherited

4. H. A. Kennedy, "The Hellenistic Atmosphere of the Epistle of James," *Expositor,* v. 2, 1911; J. Moffat, (MNTC) *The General Epistles* (London: Hodder & Stroughton, 1948).

5. Laws, *Commentary on St. James,* pp. 37ff.

6. So J. B. Adamson, *James: The Man and His Message* (Grand Rapids: Eerdmans, 1989); P. Maynard-Reid, *Poverty and Wealth in James* (Maryknoll, N.Y.: Orbis Books, 1987).

7. Thus Peter Davids's (NIGTC) *The Epistle of James* (Grand Rapids: Eerdmans, 1982).

8. E.g., M. Dibelius, in his influential commentary, *Der Brief der Jakobus* (Goettingen: Vandenhoeck & Ruprecht, 1920), Eng. ed. tr. H. Greeven, *James* (Philadelphia: Fortress Press, 1976).

instruction. On the other hand, those who regard the author as significantly ordering, editing, expanding, and adapting his material naturally suppose that something of his particular interests and concerns, or the general issues facing his readers, may be read from these indications of his redaction.[9]

This debate has particular significance for understanding the extensive material on wealth and poverty in James. Those who think of the author as simply handing on an eclectic and unstructured body of teaching tend to regard this material as part of a traditional association between piety and poverty. This they take to have purely poetic or religious meaning, unrelated to the actual economic circumstances of those within and outside the community. In their view, James is using the terms "poor" and "rich" as virtual synonyms for "pious" and "wicked," or even for "member" and "outsider," and nothing about the economic status of Christians or about the moral status of wealth may be learned from its teaching.[10] Instead, the condemnations of wealth are to be understood as blanket judgments on unbelievers.

Conversely, those who see the author as importantly selecting, interpreting, and ordering the tradition for his own purposes tend to assume that the focus on wealth and its dangers and abuses indicates an actual problem of concern either to the writer or to his expected audience. These interpreters generally argue that the economic terms are to be taken literally, and that the tradition of the pious poor is invoked by the writer to give weight and emphasis to his treatment of real practical and ethical issues arising within his congregations.[11]

Because of its immediate implications for the interpretation of our text, this question cannot be sidestepped. It has already been acknowledged that data about the historical situation of James's epistle are inconclusive. Nonetheless I am convinced, based on the internal logic of the moral

9. So a variety of commentators, including Laws, *Commentary on St. James;* Davids, *Epistle of James;* P. Maynard-Reid, *Poverty and Wealth in James.*

10. See Dibelius, *Brief der Jakobus,* pp. 39-45 and 235ff.; James Moffat, *The General Epistles* (London: Hodder & Stoughton, 1948), p. 33; Franz Mussner, *Der Jakobsbrief* (Freiburg: *Herders Theologischer Kommentar zum Neuen Testament,* Herder, 1967).

11. Some of these commentators take this as evidence for a mid-first-century date and a Palestinian location for the writing of the letter, but data about the economic circumstances of the period are so scanty and open to such diverse interpretation that it can only be said that such an ascription is possible.

arguments in James, that the material on wealth and poverty is to be taken at face value as addressing questions of the moral and religious status of wealth. Furthermore, while I recognize the existence of a traditional association between poverty and piety in the Old Testament and intertestamental literature, I regard it as an impoverishment of at least the canonical tradition to strip it of its concrete material reference. The tradition that James invokes is not merely poetic or rhetorical, but a vigorous and sensitive *moral* tradition: its incorporation strengthens the ethical force and relevance of the epistle's teaching. I will explicate and defend these views below, in the analysis of 5:1-6 and related passages.

Finally, it seems appropriate to say a word about the literary and theological character of this much-maligned epistle. Some modern scholars[12] agree with the famous disparagements of Luther, "a chaos!" and "an epistle of straw."[13] Even a relatively appreciative commentator like Laws remarks, "By contrast with thinkers such as Paul, John, or the author of Hebrews, the Christology of James must inevitably be judged as superficial and undeveloped,"[14] and she finds it to "move from one subject to another with only a loose train of thought discernible."[15] Others find "a writing of rare vigor and life which interprets [the faith] in a manner both distinctive and compelling,"[16] and call the canonical text "carefully constructed."[17]

On the matter of the literary character and cohesiveness of the letter, at least a tentative assessment is required, since how one views the whole of the letter will affect how one understands individual passages. I find unpersuasive the claims of the proponents of form criticism that James is merely traditional parenesis, composed of a series of standard maxims joined by catchwords with no particular order or structure. This reading ignores both the connections between the topics that are developed within

12. E.g., Dibelius, *Brief der Jakobus,* and G. Bornkamm, *Die Religion in Geschichte und Gegenwart* II, 1958, who find James "virtually without Christian content" or intelligible order.

13. *LW,* 35:362; 354.

14. *Commentary on St. James,* p. 3.

15. Ibid., p. 7.

16. L. T. Johnson, *The Writings of the New Testament: An Interpretation* (Philadelphia: Fortress Press, 1986), p. 453. See also his "The Use of Leviticus 19 in the Epistle of James," *Journal of Biblical Literature* 101, 1982, pp. 391-401.

17. Davids, *Epistle of James,* p. 25.

the epistle (e.g., between faith, wisdom, and purity of life), and the recurrences of particular subjects throughout the letter (most saliently, our topic of wealth and possessions).[18]

Several scholars have noted the way in which the first chapter introduces themes that are picked up and expanded later in the epistle.[19] A few have proposed more detailed accounts of the structure of the letter.[20] While some of the details of these analyses seem to strain for connections that are not readily apparent, they are persuasive enough in general to justify the claim that the epistle has both internal coherence and progressive development of particular topics. On balance, I accept Davids's general view that the letter is a body of homiletical material incorporating traditional parenesis and modifying it to address topics of particular concern to the writer. It is broadly structured around the topics of enduring trials, the necessity of singleness of heart, and the dangers posed by wealth.

Judgments of the theological value of canonical texts are dubious in that they depend upon as many variables in the judge as in the text, ranging from substantive theological and moral convictions to matters of literary taste. In particular, it makes little sense to criticize the Christology of a brief letter that hardly touches upon Christological questions at all. Arguments from silence are precarious indeed. The point made by Luke Johnson[21] that it would be more appropriate to compare James with Romans 12–13 than Romans 3–5, with Ephesians 4–6 than Ephesians 1–3, is well taken. As a piece of ethical instruction James is vigorous and thought provoking, and its view of "faith made perfect in action" (2:22) preserves a vital element in Christian understanding.

18. Dibelius actually argues (*Brief der Jakobus,* p. 11) that such recurrences are merely repetitions of identical ideas, and indicate the absence of logical arrangement, a characteristic of parenesis understood as the simple handing-on of traditional maxims. This seems to me to flatten the text by failing to attend to important distinctions as well as to the nuances of relationship. The exhortation against preferential treatment for the rich in 2:1-13 is related to the warning about the transience of wealth (1:9-11), as to the excoriation of the rich in 5:1-6, but it is not believably a simple repetition, a sign that the author did not notice that he had already talked about rich people somewhere else.

19. Johnson, *Writings of the NT,* p. 456; J. B. Adamson, *James: The Man and His Message* (Grand Rapids: Eerdmans, 1989), p. 20; Davids, *Epistle of James,* pp. 25-28.

20. Adamson, *James: Man and Message,* pp. 81-99; Davids, *Epistle of James,* pp. 22-29.

21. *Writings of the NT,* p. 456.

Text, Translation, and Boundaries

The Greek manuscript tradition of James's epistle is fairly unified but rather late, with the earliest complete texts dating from the fourth century. Our pericope contains only one textual variant of any significance,[22] which does not substantially alter the sense of the passage.

The following translation follows the UBS text, and is intended to be as literal as possible.

1 Come now, you rich [men], begin to weep, crying aloud over your miseries which are coming upon you.
2 Your wealth has rotted, and your garments have become moth-eaten;
3 Your gold and silver have become covered with rust, and their rust will be for a witness against you, and will eat your flesh like fire. You have stored up treasure in the last days.
4 Behold, the wages of the laborers who mowed your fields, the ones you kept by fraud, cry out; and the cries of the reapers have entered the ears of the Lord of Hosts.
5 You have lived in luxury on the earth, and in self-indulgence; you fattened your hearts in a day of slaughter.
6 You have condemned and murdered the righteous [man]; he does not resist you.

Some commentators, responding to the causal connective οὖν (therefore) in verse 7, treat this passage as part of a longer discourse (5:1-11) on the eschatological vindication of the suffering poor (whether literal or figurative). Although I recognize that the connection between these texts is crucial to interpreting both of them, I will deal with this relationship under the heading of the context of our passage in the epistle.

22. In v. 4, where ἀπεστερημένος (having been stolen or taken by fraud) is replaced in a few manuscripts by ἀφυστερημένος (having been withheld).

Reading the Indictment

This short passage is so dense with allusions and quoted fragments from the Old Testament and Apocrypha that it cannot fully be understood apart from the traditions on which it draws. Not only do they help to identify the genre and intended addressees of the text but they form an essential part of the moral and literary framework that the epistle assumes and brings to bear on its readers.

Verse 1

The passage begins with the same rhetorical imperative as in 4:13, ἄγε νῦν ("Come now"), so that the address is in the second person and formally direct. However, both the uncompromising judgment the passage renders and its use of the vocabulary characteristic of the prophetic denunciations indicate that this text is addressed not to those within the community, but to outsiders. The sins that are condemned are spoken of in past tenses, while the eschatological day of judgment is so near as to be spoken of partly in the present tense. For all that, there is no word of moral exhortation, no call to repentance, no imperative at all save the one that bids the rich to weep for their imminent misery. (The injunction to "cry aloud" [ὀλολύζοντες] is particularly characteristic of the Septuagint's translation of Isaiah,[23] where it introduces oracles against the nations.) This is not an effort to change the behavior of the rich who are addressed, but the announcement of a sentence already passed.[24]

The fierceness and the apparent generality of the address here, directed as it has seemed to the rich per se, has given rise to the school of thought already mentioned[25] that takes this passage to represent the tradition of the "pious poor," and thus not to refer to the actual material status or economic ethics of the Christian community. But such an interpretation requires that this verse be read in isolation, ignoring the particulars of the

23. Cf. 13:6, 14:31, 22:12, etc.

24. Contrast the address in the passage that follows immediately, 5:7-11: "Therefore, brothers [and sisters]. . . ." Here the imminence of the eschatological day provides a foundation for encouragement and moral exhortation.

25. See pp. 93-94.

case made in verses 2-6 against the rich who are thus condemned. This strategy disregards both the immediate context in James and the general pattern of oracles of judgment, in which the announcement of condemnation is regularly followed by the description of the sins that make judgment just and inevitable.[26] Such an arbitrary reading cannot be justified. This verse must be taken as the declaration of a coming judgment whose rationale follows immediately.

Verses 2-3

The description of the riches of the wealthy as "rotted" and of their garments as "moth-eaten" is rich and evocative. It recalls a series of Old Testament texts in which these motifs of decay symbolize the transience and corruptibility of wealth and of human life in general, and their susceptibility to divine judgment.[27]

The metaphorical figure of gold and silver as rusting has an illuminating parallel in Sirach 29: "Lose your silver for the sake of a brother . . . and do not let it rust under a stone and be lost" (v. 10). Instead, the chapter continues, "Lay up treasure according to the commandments of the Most High. . . . Store up almsgiving in your treasury" (vv. 11-12). Here rust is symbolic of the useless inactivity of hoarded wealth, and is evidence that the owner has neglected the duty of almsgiving. This is the "witness against you" predicted in James 5:3. The "rust" on the gold and silver testifies that the rich have not given alms but have "hoarded treasure in the last days," days of trouble and of judgment.[28] Finally, therefore, the rust is spoken of as a means of punishment: it will "eat your flesh like fire."

This is the first accusation against the rich: they have let their accumulated wealth sit idle, and given nothing to the poor.

26. Is. 10:5-19, 29:1-24; Jer. 50:1-13; etc.

27. E.g., Job 13:28; Ps. 39:11; Is. 50:9, 51:8.

28. The same tradition, obviously, shapes the texts in Matthew 6:19-20 and Luke 12:33, which refer to treasures rusting or destroyed by moths: they represent wealth that is accumulated rather than being given as alms and thus converted to treasure in heaven. A number of such motifs are common to James and the Q material, particularly as it appears in Matthew. Some have raised the issue of a possible literary relationship between James and Matthew, an interesting question that is (unfortunately) beyond the scope of this work.

Verse 4

Where the preceding verses draw on the prophets and the Wisdom tradition, this text adds the laws of Leviticus and Deuteronomy to the list of moral sources. The specific concern that the wages of day laborers not be withheld arose in a context where the status of hireling belonged to the poor whose familial land had been sold or otherwise alienated due to debt. Thus Leviticus 19:13 forbids keeping wages back even from sundown until the next morning, and Deuteronomy 24:15 adds the explanation, "You shall give [the laborer] his hire on the day he earns it, for he is poor and sets his heart upon it, lest he cry against you to the Lord, and it be accounted sin in you." The stringency and importance of these regulations is amplified in another text from Sirach: "To take away a neighbor's living is to murder him; to deprive an employee of his wages is to shed blood" (34:26-27).

Both the law and its amplification are recalled by James's figure of the stolen wages that cry out, evoking as it does the passage in Genesis 4:10 where the blood of murdered Abel cries out from the ground for vindication. The cries of the defrauded workers have ascended to God's ears, and the appellation "the Lord of Hosts," evoking the "God of Battles" who fights to vindicate his people, hints at the vengeance that will overtake those who have robbed the poor of their very means of survival.

This is the second accusation against the wealthy: they have acquired and maintained their wealth through injustice, by depriving the poor of payment for their labor.

Verse 5

Here the rich are described as luxury-loving and self-indulgent, busy with feeding and carousing even on the very "day of slaughter." This phrase, taken from Jeremiah 12:3, refers to the day of God's judgment on the "wicked who prosper" and "all the faithless who live at ease" (Jer. 12:1). The depiction of the rich as living sumptuously "on the earth" contrasts with the suffering and want inflicted by their lack of generosity and justice, as well as with the misery of the eschatological day that is coming upon them.

Here is the third accusation against the rich: they are self-preoccupied and heedless of God, absorbed like cattle at the trough even as judgment approaches.

Verse 6

James's indictment reaches its climax here. The rich are said to have pronounced judgment against (κατεδικάσατε) the innocent and executed them, bringing to mind the excoriations of the prophets against those who pervert the judicial process (Amos 5:11; Is. 5:23, 10:1-3; etc.). An even closer parallel may be found in Wisdom 2, where the wealthy who are powerful (vv. 6-9) plot to oppress the righteous one who is poor and weak (vv. 10-11), concluding, "Let us condemn him to a shameful death" (v. 20). From the virtual murder of stealing earned bread from the poor, the charge has come to murder outright; the wealthy have turned the very machinery of justice into an instrument of their power, against which the innocent are helpless.

Thus James levels a fourth and final accusation: the rich are guilty of judicial murder.

It is worth noting that these charges are not a general list of sufferings that any wicked person might impose on any righteous one. Rather, they are specific acts made possible by the concrete circumstance of great disparities in wealth and in the power that accrues with wealth. As I have indicated, the fact that each of these charges is expressed in language drawn from the Scriptural tradition has been used to argue that they are *merely* traditional and spiritualized, and do not reflect anything of the actual situation and experience of the writer and his readers. However, both the immediate context of this passage in the epistle and the treatment that the topic of wealth receives elsewhere in the letter refute that argument.

5:1-6 in Context

While there are strong indications that James 5:1-6 is addressed to those outside the Christian community, it is quite clear that 5:7-11 is addressed to those within it. Whether ἀδελφοί is translated "brothers" or "brothers and sisters," it is James's familiar designation for the believers to whom he writes (1:2, 1:16, 1:19, etc.). Thus it is particularly revealing that this following passage begins with the causal connective οὖν; "*Therefore,* be patient, brothers [and sisters], until the coming of the Lord." If, as "therefore" implies, this counsel of patience is justified by the promise of God's judgment against the rich that has preceded it, then it must be addressed to those who have suffered at the hands of the rich: that is, to the poor who have been ignored or defrauded or even falsely condemned by the wealthy. The communities to which James writes must include at least some such persons, who have suffered real harms as the result of real economic circumstances.

That James appeals to the experience of his readers when he speaks of injustices done to the poor is confirmed by another direct address in 2:6-7. Here, arguing against preferential treatment for the wealthy, he asks rhetorically, "Is it not the rich who oppress you . . . who drag you into court . . . who blaspheme the honorable name which is invoked over you?" Such rhetoric would make no sense at all if it were *not* an appeal to his readers' experience. The idea that this text reflects a merely traditional association between wealth and wrongdoing is untenable.

However, there is another way of reading this passage, which is only too ready to infer the socioeconomic status of the letter's writer and readers from its moral pronouncements. On this view, the accusations against the rich in James are simply an expression of the *ressentiment* of the poor against the affluent, part of an unhealthy attempt to give positive moral and religious value to the circumstance of poverty. Read thus, James's indictment is an attack on wealth *as such,* and marks this text as the product of a group composed exclusively of the poor, who use the only weapons at their disposal to denigrate the status and impugn the morals of their social superiors.[29] This reading is also defeated by the remainder of the letter. For all that James speaks of the sins of the rich in general, he does not consistently treat the rich as enemies or even as *necessarily* outsiders to the community. The impassioned argument of 2:1-12 is against treating rich visitors to the church with special deference. It is *not* against admitting or even welcoming them to the assembly; rather, it presumes that they are to be admitted. There is also an apparent

29. This view is espoused by Dibelius (*Brief der Jakobus,* pp. 39-41), who understands the Old Testament tradition appropriated by James as "poverty theology," an unhealthy response to the failure of Israel's national strength. He cites Nietzsche as having characterized this development (p. 39, note 136).

reference in 1:10 to "the brother who is rich," but this is a disputed reading and must be explained.

James 1:9-10 counsels, "Let the lowly brother boast in his exaltation, and the rich in his humiliation." The correct translation of these verses is debated. The most natural reading of these parallel clauses supplies the noun ἀδελφός (brother) from verse 9 to supplement the adjective πλούσιος (rich) in verse 10, as it supplies the single verb "boast"; this gives "and the rich [brother] [boast] in his humiliation," so that both rich and poor are addressed as members of the community. The alternative reading, grammatically less likely but still possible, treats πλούσιος as a substantive, and contrasts the poor brother with the rich outsider: "let the lowly brother boast in his exaltation, and the rich [man] ["boast"] in his humiliation." The second interpretation presents a difficulty, aside from being somewhat unnatural grammatically: it requires that the single word "boast" (καυχάσθω), which is taken at face value in verse 9, be understood as heavily ironic when it is supplied in verse 10. This is not impossible, but it is strained. Commentators who prefer this reading usually give as a rationale the "harsh words of 1:10-11,"[30] which, it is said, speak of the eschatological judgment upon the rich, and offer no consolation. Such a prophecy of destruction is thought to be incompatible with an address to believers.

But it is not clear that this *is* the force of those verses. The figure of the wildflower or grass, which passes away, is familiar from the Psalms[31] and Job,[32] as well as from the very similar passage in Isaiah 40:6-8. In every case, the point is the transient and insubstantial nature of human life and human glory, and the common fate that awaits all human beings regardless of wealth or social standing. The fleeting beauty of life is contrasted with the enduring power and love of God, which are the only foundation of security. It appears that what is promised to the rich, and constitutes the ground of their humiliation, is not condemnation but *mortality.* These warnings are consistently addressed to God's people as a reminder of the vanity of judging by, or trusting in, human values and assessments. If this is the point in James, then it would suggest that the rich man's "humiliation" is his recognition of his utter dependence upon

30. Maynard-Reid, *Poverty and Wealth,* p. 41.
31. Ps. 37:2, 90:5ff., 103:15.
32. Job 14:2.

God and his lack of any special status as he faces a doom that is universal. His reliance upon God is to be the ground of his boast. Surely this is not incompatible with addressing such a person as "brother."

If this reading is correct, then James's epistle includes portrayals of the rich as members of the community and as visitors in the church, as well as portrayals of the rich as oppressors and lawbreakers. In short, it recognizes and condemns the evils and abuses that wealth occasions, without automatically equating "rich person" with "evil outsider."

The Moral Use of the Passage

I have tried to make the case that James's treatment of wealth cannot be put down to a merely traditional link between poverty and piety, or to an economic metaphor for a spiritual condition, or to an automatic condemnation of the wealthy by the poor that gives religious sanction to envy and resentment. If all of these options are excluded, then we are left with a rather disturbing alternative: a fierce declaration of God's judgment on the wealthy as *sinners,* whose wealth is accumulated and held in defiance of God's law requiring justice and compassion, and is used to pervert the structures of society to their own ends with impunity. The indictment, based on a tradition already ancient when James wrote, sounds remarkably "modern" even now.

I have said that this text is not directly addressed by James to the church, but in the manner of a prophetic diatribe is directed to the rich who are guilty of these sins. However, like the diatribe, it is clearly not written for the sake of those evildoers to whom it is addressed. Dependent as it is for its force on a reality perspective that assumes that the law of God is sovereign and the judgment of God is imminent, the passage cannot be expected to serve as a warning to those who will not accept the truthfulness of that view. While its judgments clearly *apply* universally, it is written *for the sake of* the church, and has its moral function preeminently within the Christian community, where it operates in two distinct ways.

In the first instance, it operates in the fashion implied by its author when he follows its promise of judgment with "Therefore be patient, brothers and sisters, until the coming of the Lord." That is, it serves to sustain the hope and endurance of poor Christians who are presently suffering from economic oppression and injustice, by promising that God's vindication is very near. The miseries are already "coming upon [the rich]," and indeed are so near that James tells them to start crying immediately![33] The days in which their wealth has been piled up are the "last days," and the present in which the rich have "fattened their hearts" is already the "day of slaughter" (v. 5), which is upon them.

The imminence of judgment declared in 5:1-6 is reiterated in 5:7-11. Along with citing a number of examples from ordinary life (v. 7) and from the biblical tradition (vv. 10-11) in which patience and the endurance of suffering bring rewards, James stresses the nearness of their deliverance with "the coming of the Lord is at hand" (v. 8) and "the Judge is standing at the doors" (v. 9). Finally, James appeals to their own experience of God. They are reminded that God's mercy is sure, for they themselves "have seen the purpose of the Lord" and know that God has compassion on his people.

The second way in which the text functions morally is by inculcating a particular attitude toward wealth within the community. The warning of 2:1-12 against special deference to the rich suggests that the Christians to whom James writes are at least tempted to share the positive assessment of wealth prevalent in the wider society; by contrast, it is something of an understatement to say that James's basic attitude toward wealth is one of profound suspicion. Rather than beginning from the standpoint that wealth is evidence of the industry or sagacity of the rich, or is at least morally neutral, James begins from the assumption that wealth commonly comes from and begets corruption. He recognizes the deep ambiguity of the enormous social power wealth bestows, power both for wrongdoing and for avoiding the consequences of wrongdoing. And he takes for granted the tendency of riches to preoccupy the minds and distort the priorities of their possessors. Thus, James's picture of the moral character of wealth and God's judgment upon it counters the conventional evaluation of wealth as enviable.

Of course, in none of these observations is James an innovator; as the above rehearsal of allusions and citations within the passage has illustrated, every element in this diatribe is brought forward out of the breadth of the Jewish tradition, from law or prophets, from wisdom or apocalypse. It might be thought that James, as the purveyor of a moral tradition to which the church is already heir through the Old Testament,

33. κλαύσατε is the aorist inceptive, translated "begin to weep."

has nothing to offer contemporary Christians in the area of the moral status of wealth. But James is notably selective in what he appropriates. Nowhere to be seen is that aspect of the wisdom tradition that treats poverty as the consequence of idleness and wealth as the fruit of prudence and hard work (e.g., Prov. 6:6-11, 10:4-5, 20:13, 21:17, 20), nor the retributionist moral theory that treats all such circumstances, good or ill, as rewards for virtue or punishments for vice, so that wealth is a sign of God's favor, as poverty is a sign of his wrath (e.g., Job 36:5-12; Prov. 10:3, 10:22, 21:21, 22:4).[34]

Furthermore, James's indictment contains features that may surprise us, despite their lack of originality. In view of the seriousness of the charges of judicial murder (5:6) and fraudulent labor practices that amount to stealing bread from the poor (5:4), perhaps the severity of the promised judgment upon them comes as no surprise. But we are not accustomed to think of the other two charges as properly crimes at all; while most people regard charitable giving as praiseworthy, few regard its absence as culpable, much less actually punishable. Similarly, although some might find fault with the judgment or even the taste of those who live in luxury, few would treat their self-gratification as a serious offense. In general, even those within the church regard the disposal of income beyond what is needed to meet basic financial obligations as a matter of individual choice, and any material "lifestyle" that can be supported as morally acceptable. Thus it is instructive to note that James's first accusation is simply that the rich have heaped up possessions rather than giving them as alms.

The way that this text can function in the life of contemporary churches will vary with the situation in which they find themselves. Just as the Marcan text we examined in chapter 3 may operate quite straightforwardly to sustain the joy of Christians who have suffered losses as the price of faithfulness to Christ,[35] James may serve to support the patience and the confidence of Christians suffering poverty and oppression in our own day. But its promise of judgment can operate in another fashion as well.

The "Judge standing at the door" (5:9) who is a reminder of God's speedy vindication is also invoked by James to support the injunction to

34. For a further discussion of the Old Testament treatment of wealth, and its partial appropriation in the New Testament, see ch. 8, pp. 121-27 below.

35. See above, p. 56.

those within the church, "do not murmur against one another." In the same way, the catalogue of the sins of wealth and their consequences may serve to awaken affluent Christians of today to the seriousness of what is discreetly called "the social problem" and to the fact that God condemns injustice in distribution as well as injustice in accrual, lack of generosity as well as fraud. Along with the grounds for an alternative, "countercultural" evaluation of the meaning of wealth, it can provide alternative norms and standards for contemporary Christians' legitimate holding and use of possessions.

Even more directly than has been the case with other texts we have considered, the capacity of this passage to perform either of these moral functions within the contemporary church depends upon the acceptance of the eschatological realm toward which it looks as real in some fashion. Once again this "coming of the Lord" may be understood in a variety of ways, and the promised judgment of God may be thought to take any of a number of forms: but it is essential that it is God's judgment that is invoked, and not a merely human consequence or judgment of moral disapproval. The whole weight of James's indictment falls on the wealthy as despising God and God's law in their injustice toward the poor; what he threatens them with is not revolution or economic failure or social disapprobation, but the coming of the Lord of Hosts.

CHAPTER 7

Canonical Context

In the preceding chapters, I have examined texts chosen to represent the treatment of wealth and possessions in their respective sources. Accordingly, I looked at individual texts not only as they fit within their immediate literary contexts but (where possible) as they fit into the broader theological concerns of their various authors. Thus, for example, we viewed Luke's story of the man who had great possessions in its relation to the treatment of possessions throughout the Lucan corpus and in relation to Luke's account of the banishing of fear occasioned by Jesus' advent. Similarly, we considered Paul's assumption of equality as the natural standard for giving between local Christian communities in two ways: as part of the theme of God's overflowing grace in II Corinthians and as an expression of Paul's overriding concern for the tangible realization of Christian unity evident throughout his letters. In light of these considerations, we have formed some picture of each of these distinct sources' contributions to a Christian ethic of possessions.

But this picture, though essential, is not sufficient. In keeping with the first principle of method laid down in Part I, in order to assess the contribution of the New Testament to contemporary economic ethics, we must take account of all the sources and texts that treat the topic. Obviously, a similarly detailed reading of every New Testament text that might be thought relevant would fill several books, making the whole unmanageably long and cumbersome. Instead, I have tried in the foregoing to demonstrate the kind of close reading that is necessary to interpret New Testament texts in a way that can contribute to moral reflection in the contemporary church.

Now it remains to review and summarize in a more general way the material on wealth and possessions that is encountered in each of the other major strands of New Testament literature. We will be trying still in this briefer compass to take some account of the context and function of any explicit teaching on wealth. In this way the wider canon will provide a check upon, and a context of interpretation for, the results of the preceding studies. To the voices of Mark and Luke, Paul and James, we must add the voices of Matthew and John, and those of the authors of the deutero-Pauline tradition and of the other general epistles.

The intention here is not to cite every text that might be thought relevant, but rather to give a sample broad and representative enough to convey the moral and theological understanding of wealth and possessions presented in the canonical materials from these remaining sources. Nonetheless, the intention *is* to be responsive to the whole of the New Testament canon, and it will rightly be accounted a fault if the summaries to be offered ignore or contradict any significant aspect of the various traditions. Because the selection of relevant passages is part of the act of interpretation, a list of passages that I take to relate more or less directly to the moral status of possessions (whether they are cited or not) is appended.[1]

Matthew

It is a commonplace to observe that the Gospel of Matthew displays less interest in the issue of material wealth or poverty than does that of Luke. This is true as far as it goes, and may be seen in any number of differences in the treatment of traditions found in both gospels,[2] as well as in the absence from Matthew's gospel of much of the extensive Lucan material concerning wealth.[3] Thus it is somewhat startling to see how much remains

1. Of course, it is possible to construe the matter of relevance so broadly that virtually the whole canon becomes "relevant," from God's creation of the world to its eventual redemption in the New Jerusalem. This is entirely appropriate for some purposes, for example in the formation of a comprehensive "theology of the material world." My own aims are much more modest, and my construal of relevance correspondingly more narrow. While I will touch upon questions of the impact of the doctrine of creation on our topic, these are occasioned by texts that deal more directly with wealth and poverty, to which I limit my attention.

2. E.g., compare Mt. 3:7-12 with Lk. 3:7-17; Mt. 5:3, 6 with Lk. 6:20-21.

3. E.g., in Luke see 1:51-53; 10:33-37; 12:16-21; 16:19-31; etc.

on the topic and to note how generally suspicious of wealth are the traditions Matthew preserves.

Some half dozen references to poverty or wealth appear within Matthew's narrative, apart from Jesus' recorded teachings. The first (and almost the only positive) mention of material wealth or treasure in the gospel is of the treasures of the wise men (2:11), from which gifts are laid at the feet of the infant Jesus as an offering. Nothing further concerning the material status of any of the other figures in the narrative is said until 3:4, where John the Baptist is pictured living the life of an ascetic, clothed in camel's hair and living on a diet of locusts and wild honey.

Among the passages found in Luke that are absent from Matthew is the "inaugural speech" of Luke 4:16-19, in which Jesus quotes Isaiah to identify the preaching of good news to the poor as part of his ministry. However, Matthew does preserve the similar passage (11:2-5) where Jesus answers John's question, "Are you the one?" by saying "The poor have good news preached to them," confirming that this is one of the signs of the Messianic age. Both Jesus and the disciples are depicted as poor, and it is to the disciples who have "left everything to follow" that eternal life is promised (19:27-29). Jesus warns the teacher who would follow him of the conditions of that loyalty: "Foxes have holes, and birds have nests, but the Son of Man has nowhere to lay his head" (8:20). But even as we observed in Luke, so also in Matthew we find nothing as simple as a rule requiring material poverty, or equating wealth with unrighteousness. As Jesus' birth was marked by the recognition and worship of the wealthy magi, so his death is marked by the recognition and service of a wealthy man named Joseph, who places Jesus' body in his own tomb (27:57-60) and vanishes from the story.

Most of Matthew's explicit instruction on wealth and possessions is concentrated in the Sermon on the Mount (chs. 5–7), in which three distinct themes are addressed. The first is the necessity of giving alms and the appropriate manner and motive for doing so. The traditional duty of almsgiving is intensified with the injunction, "Give to everyone who begs from you" (5:42), and this is followed by warnings against giving done publicly "in order to be praised"; such donors, Jesus says, "have received their reward" (6:2-4).[4]

4. Reflecting Matthew's consistent interest in purity of motive, this material is unique to Matthew.

The second topic addressed in the Sermon is the possibility and importance of trusting God to meet the material needs of life. Followers are told to pray for daily bread (6:11) and in general to ask for whatever is needed (7:7-11). They are to have no anxiety concerning food or clothing (6:25, 31), since anxiety is neither necessary nor productive (6:26-29), but are to place God's kingdom above all these considerations, and be assured that God will provide what they need (6:33).[5]

The third theme concerning possessions in Matthew's Sermon is the peril of accumulating wealth. "Do not lay up for yourself treasures on earth" (6:19), Jesus' followers are warned, for "where your treasure is, there will your heart be" (6:21). And immediately thereafter, Jesus flatly states, "No one can serve two masters. . . . You cannot serve God and riches" (6:24).

Only three other texts preserved in Matthew directly address the moral and spiritual status of wealth or the appropriate use of possessions. Two of these return to the theme of the dangers posed by wealth, and the last presents yet more forcefully the strictness of the duty to give alms noted above.

On the former topic there is the interpretation of the parable of the sower (13:18-23), found in similar form in all three synoptic gospels. Here it is "the deceitfulness of wealth" (13:22) that chokes the implanted word of God and renders it unfruitful. A similar theme is treated in Matthew's story of the rich young man (19:16-29). Matthew's version of the story differs in several respects from those in Mark and Luke,[6] most importantly for our purposes in the way in which it answers the question of what is lacking in the one who is obedient to the commandments. The substance of the reply Jesus gives is identical to that in Mark 10:21: go, sell your possessions, follow me. However, in Matthew this is given not as an

5. This material is, of course, parallel to what we considered in Luke 12, with some suggestive redactional differences that space does not permit us to pursue.

6. To begin with, Matthew's young man (he is so identified in 19:20 and 22) asks a somewhat different question: "What good action must I do to inherit eternal life?" He does not address Jesus as "Good" (although Jesus answers him as if he had — v. 17); and in response to Jesus' rather different answer, "If you would enter life, keep the commandments" (v. 17), he asks, "Which?" (v. 18). The list Jesus provides differs from that recorded in Mark; gone is the anomalous "do not defraud" (Mk. 10:19), and to the standard second table of the Decalogue is added Lev. 19:18: "Love your neighbor as yourself." The whole tenor of the conversation here is different, resembling more a discussion about the priorities of the Torah (cf. Mt. 22:35-40) than a conversation about what is required for eternal life. As in Mark and Luke, the man reports that he has obeyed all these commands, but here he is the one who implies that this is inadequate, asking, "What do I still lack?" (v. 20).

imperative but rather as advice, with a preface that has given rise to the traditional category of supererogatory actions called "counsels of perfection": "If you would be perfect, go, sell your possessions, and you will have treasure in heaven; and come follow me" (19:21).

The striking thing about the story is that the comment Jesus offers after the young man's refusal is virtually identical in Matthew (19:24) to that in Mark and Luke: "It is easier for a camel to go through the eye of a needle than for a rich man to enter the kingdom of God." Although Matthew has framed this story as an exchange about the conditions conducive to moral perfection, the retention of the original ending of the story suggests an understanding at odds with the usual interpretation. Apparently the "perfection" made possible by poverty is virtually necessary for those who would enter the kingdom. It suggests that in Matthew's view, perfection itself is not "supererogatory," but is simply that to which Jesus' followers are called. (Cf. Mt. 5:20 and 5:48.)

The third and final instruction on wealth and possessions outside the Sermon on the Mount returns to the first topic of almsgiving. In the parable of the sheep and the goats (25:31-46), the obligation to provide materially for the poor among the brethren[7] and the consequences of failing to do so are laid out as starkly as possible: "Depart from me, you cursed . . . for I was hungry and you gave me nothing to eat, I was thirsty and you gave me nothing to drink, I was a stranger and you did not invite me in, I was naked and you did not clothe me" (vv. 41-42).

Thus we have seen that Matthew's gospel retains the tradition that Jesus and his followers were materially poor, and several passages suggest that their abandonment of possessions and the settled life they entail was

7. The reference here is to 25:41-43, but the intended scope of the parable is not completely clear. On one hand, the parallel declaration to the righteous includes the statement, "Inasmuch as you did it to one of the least of my brothers (ἀδελφῶν μου), you did it to me" (25:40). Although ἀδελφός is not used in Matthew uniquely and consistently of believers, it is often used in that way, and the possessive pronoun is particularly suggestive (e.g., 12:48-50, 23:9). On the other hand, this parable is explicitly given as a model of the judging of the nations, and the declaration to the condemned speaks only of not having cared for "the least of these" (25:45), which might be taken universally. In view of the similar passage in 10:40-42, where receiving a disciple is explicitly the same as receiving Christ, it is probably best to interpret the parable as having in view the needy within the Christian community. Nevertheless, there is some ambiguity. (The broader question of differential duties to community members and nonmembers will be discussed in chapters 8 and 9.)

a condition of their ministry. One of the characteristic aspects of that ministry, which identified Jesus as the Messiah, was the preaching of good news to the poor. There is accordingly a particular focus on the perils of wealth, both as a hindrance to discipleship and as an alternative object of loyalty and service.

Matthew preserves the dominical sayings about the needlessness and futility of anxiety about material needs in connection with exhortations to trust in God's provision and to "seek first [God's] kingdom and righteousness." Thus Jesus' followers are not to lay up treasures on earth "where moth and rust consume,"[8] but to gain "treasure in heaven," a figure for almsgiving in the wisdom tradition. Finally, the stringency and importance of the requirement of sharing goods with the needy is underscored by the parable of the sheep and the goats, in which care for the poor among the community is identified with care for Jesus himself, and made the test for entrance to the kingdom.

The Johannine Tradition

The Gospel of John, with its overwhelming focus on the identity and authority of Jesus as the Christ, is notable for its lack of explicit attention to questions of wealth and possessions.[9] At the same time, however, more than any other gospel it focuses on the love that both binds and identifies Jesus' true disciples. To love Jesus is to obey his commands (14:15, 21, 23-24; 15:9-10, 14), and preeminent among them is the command to "love one another," which occurs no fewer than four times (14:34, 35; 15:12, 17). The model for the disciples' love for each other is to be the love of Jesus for them, and its ultimate test is the willingness to sacrifice: "Greater love has no one than this, that a man lay down his life for his friends" (15:13). Jesus' repeated prayer for the disciples is that they may be one as he and the Father are one (17:11, 21, 22-23).

The concrete expression of this love and unity in the life of the church has already been suggested in the gospel by the story of Jesus washing the disciples' feet (13:1-17). John introduces the narrative with

8. Cf. the interpretation of James, p. 98.

9. Even where parallels with the synoptics occur, as with the figure of Joseph of Arimathea (19:38), references to economic status are absent.

"Having loved his own who were in the world, he loved them to the end" (13:1), and draws the moral explicitly at the conclusion: "If I then . . . have washed your feet, you also ought to wash one another's feet. For I have given you an example, that you should do as I have done to you" (13:14-15). Love, then, is to take the form of practical service.

The particular implications of Christian love for those who are in material need are made perfectly explicit in I John. Having already identified love of the community as the infallible sign of genuine love for God (2:9-11; 3:11-15; see also 4:7-12, 20-21), the epistle adds, "By this we have known love, that one laid down his life for us; and we ought to lay down our lives for our brothers [and sisters]" (3:16). Thus the reality of love is easy to test: "Whoever has the [means of] worldly life, and sees his brother in need, yet shuts his heart against him, how does God's love remain in him? Little children, let us love not in words on the tongue, but in action and in truth" (3:17-18). To pass this test is to stand confident and assured before God (3:19-23); to fail it is to reveal that one still dwells in darkness (2:9) and in death (3:14).

Finally, the conflict between love for one's sisters and brothers and love of the goods of the world is understood as absolute and ineradicable. The obverse of love for the community is that one *not* love "the world and the things that are in the world" (2:15), a phrase denoting not the world as creation but the world as it stands in pride and rebellion against God: the world that falls under judgment and passes away (2:16-17). Love for the world thus understood stands directly opposed to love for God, so that "if anyone does love the world, the love of the Father is not in him" (2:15).

In the Apocalypse the writer gives a striking illustration of the spiritual peril of prizing worldly wealth rather than the riches of faith. In the most severe of all the Spirit's words to the various churches, the church at Laodicea (3:14-19) is described as "lukewarm" and said to be in danger of being "vomited out." However, the worst of it is that they are unaware of their danger. In fact, they are full of a proud self-sufficiency generated by prosperity: "You say, 'I am rich, I have become wealthy and need nothing,' and you do not know that you are wretched and pitiable and poor and blind and naked" (3:17). They are counseled to buy true gold from Christ (3:18 — an apparent reference to the spiritual wealth of salvation: cf. 2:9), and called upon to accept chastisement, returning to fellowship with Jesus (3:19-20).

Greed for wealth and luxury are also among the sins for which Babylon is condemned. Her fall is vividly depicted in the visions of chapters 17 and 18, where the city appears as a woman "dressed in purple and scarlet . . . glittering with gold, precious stones, and pearls" (17:4). Her appetite for self-indulgence is suggested by the catalogue of expensive goods, from spices to slaves, that will flow into her no more (18:11-13). Lamenting her fall are the greedy merchants who "grew rich from her excessive luxuries" (18:3); they "stand far off, terrified at her torment," and mourn that "such great wealth is brought to ruin" (18:15-17).

But despite his deep suspicion of worldly wealth, elsewhere in the Apocalypse the author is quite ready to use these same symbols of material richness and luxury to convey the beauty and power of God's reign in the New Jerusalem. The Heavenly City is pictured "coming down from Heaven arrayed like a bride" (Rev. 21:2), with streets of pure gold and gates of precious stones (Rev. 21:18-21). The city where the saints will reign with God and the Lamb is a place of plenty, pictured as a restored garden of Eden, where the tree of life will yield fruit every month (Rev. 22:1-2). Even at his most dualistic, when picturing the world as divided finally into the righteous and the wicked, the writer is never actually antimaterialistic, and his dualism is not between the worlds of matter and of spirit. Fatal as an object of lust and attachment, material wealth remains a fitting adornment for the Holy City, a token of the spiritual wealth of the elect.

The Deutero-Pauline Traditions[10]

All of the many references to wealth (πλοῦτος) in Ephesians are to the riches of God's mercy (2:4), grace (2:7), and glory (3:16) revealed in Jesus Christ, through whom all the saints are "fellow heirs" (3:6) of the "wealth of his glorious inheritance" (1:18). Against the background of this "surpassing" and "immeasurable" wealth, desire for mere earthly wealth is

10. This designation reflects the majority view of contemporary scholars that regards both Colossians and Ephesians, together with the pastoral epistles, as not authentically Pauline. However, the status of Colossians in particular is still a matter of serious debate. No position on that question is espoused by its inclusion in this category, as the question is beyond the scope of my present research.

revealed as faithless and contemptible. The greedy person (πλεονέκτης — literally "the one desiring more") is nothing short of an idolater, who has forfeited his inheritance in the kingdom (5:5). Such a sin "must not even be named among you" (5:3); it is one of the things for which "the wrath of God comes upon the sons of disobedience" (5:6). But however much greed for material goods is condemned, the legitimacy and necessity of working for one's livelihood is affirmed, with the important stipulation that even this is motivated by generosity; the former thief is to "labor, doing good work with his own hands *so that* (ἵνα) he may be able to share with those in need" (4:28).

The same themes are touched upon more briefly in the letter to the Colossians. Here the "riches" are the glory, wisdom, and knowledge of God in Christ (1:27; 2:3) on one hand, and the Colossians' understanding of the mystery of Christ on the other (2:2). In the assurance of their possession of this mystery, the Colossians are to "put to death what is earthly in [them]," including "greed, which is idolatry" (3:5). As in Ephesians, covetousness is identified as one of the sins bringing God's judgment (3:6). Nevertheless, the worth of labor is again affirmed, this time with the injunction to regard all such service, even that rendered in slavery, as given to Christ: "whatever your task, work heartily. . . . You are serving the Lord Christ" (3:23-24; cf. Titus 2:9-10; 3:1).

The pastoral epistles share the same severe judgment on greed or avarice, there usually called φιλαργυρία (literally "the love of money"). Freedom from this vice is given as a condition of selection for the office of bishop (I Tim. 3:3; see also Titus 1:7), and in II Timothy the love of money is included in the list of vices that will mark the evil last days (3:2). The writer of I Timothy offers what is almost a homily on the dangers of avarice (6:6-12), warning that those who desire to be rich "fall into a snare, and into senseless and dangerous desires that cause them to sink into ruin and destruction" (6:9). He even goes so far as to say that "the love of money is a root of all evils" (6:10). The righteous are to shun all such cravings, and be content with food and clothing, aiming their desires at "righteousness, piety, faith, love, endurance and gentleness" (6:11).

Nevertheless, there is no blanket condemnation of wealth as such; Timothy is given a charge for those who are "rich in the present age" (I Tim. 6:17-19), which indicates that they are understood as part of the community. The rich are exhorted not to be arrogant and not to "set their hopes on the uncertainty of wealth" (6:17); instead they are to be "rich in good works," by their generosity "treasuring up a good foundation so that they may lay hold on the true life" (6:18-19). As in Ephesians and Colossians, there is a concern that Christians be financially responsible and self-supporting, and especially that they provide materially for their own households. Such support is an act of piety acceptable to God (I Tim. 5:4), and refusal to provide it is tantamount to denying the faith. Such a person is "worse than an unbeliever," having failed in a duty recognized even among pagans (I Tim. 5:8).

The General Epistles

The epistle to the Hebrews offers an argument sustained over twelve chapters, laying out the superior excellence of the salvation made available through faith in Christ. Its repeated exhortations to faith and faithfulness are interspersed with general moral encouragements and followed by a variety of specific practical injunctions in chapter 13.

Chapter 10 includes an extended call to steadfastness and endurance under persecution. In this setting, the readers are reminded of how they "joyfully accepted the confiscation of [their] property, because [they] knew of better and lasting possessions" (10:34). The general admonition to "let brotherly love continue" (13:1), which opens chapter 13, is specified in a number of imperatives, beginning with "do not neglect hospitality" (v. 2). In addition, the church is to "be mindful of those in prison . . . and of the ill-treated," and here the writer appeals to the most general ground of sympathy for the suffering: Christians are to remember them simply because they share the condition of embodiedness (v. 3).

Believers are enjoined to remain free of the love of money (ἀφιλάργυρος), and to be satisfied with the things they have (13:5). The ground of this contentment is the promise of God's presence and care (13:5-6), which can sustain confidence even in the context of imprisonment and ill-treatment. This confidence and the knowledge that they have on earth "no lasting city, but seek the city which is to come" (v. 14) are the foundation of the writer's final appeal. "Do not neglect to do good and to share what you have" (v. 16); such sharing the writer calls a "sacrifice pleasing to God."

Most of the references to wealth or possessions in the Petrine letters contrast the "perishable gold" of the world with the "imperishable riches" of faith in Jesus Christ and the salvation that he offers (I Pet. 1:4, 7, 18-19). Having been given so great an inheritance (1:4, 23), the readers are to "set their hope fully on the grace to be given to [them]" (1:13) and "conform no longer to evil desires" (1:14). They are to "love one another earnestly from the heart" (1:22), and therefore to rid themselves of envy (2:1). Women are to eschew outward ornaments of gold in favor of the "inward, imperishable adornment of a gentle and quiet spirit" (3:4), and believers are to offer hospitality to one another without complaint (4:9). Finally the author addresses himself to the elders, admonishing them to "tend the flock of God among you willingly . . . not for shameful gain" (5:2).

By contrast, the false teachers against whom the epistle of II Peter rails are said to be motivated by avarice (2:3). They pervert the gospel for gain, literally "making merchandise of you by false words." He says of these false teachers that they have "hearts trained in greed" (2:14), and have followed the way of Balaam, who cursed Israel for money (2:15). A similar condemnation of heretical teachers fills much of the epistle of Jude, and the writer there gives a similar analysis of their motives. They have fallen into "the error of Balaam," to which "they have abandoned themselves for the sake of gain" (v. 11).

I will defer to the following chapter the task of ordering and summarizing the breadth and variety of the canonical witness.

Table of Passages[11]

Matthew
2:11
3:4
5:42
6:2-4
6:11
6:19-21
6:24-33
7:6-11
8:19-20
10:8-10
11:2-5
13:22
19:16-30
25:31-46
27:57-60

Mark
1:4-6
4:18-19
10:17-31
12:41-44
14:3-9

Luke
1:51-53
3:10-14
4:18-19
5:11, 28
6:20-21
6:24-25, 30
6:34-35, 38
7:19-23
8:2-3
8:14
9:2-4
10:4-7
10:33-37
11:3
11:9-11
12:15-34
14:12-14
16:1-13
16:19-31
18:18-30
19:1-10
21:1-4
22:35-36

Acts
2:44-45
4:32-37
5:1-11
20:33-35

Romans
12:6-8
12:13
15:25-27

I Corinthians
7:30
9:3-15
11:20-22
16:1-2

II Corinthians
8:1–9:15

Galatians
6:6

Ephesians
4:28
5:3, 5-6

Philippians
4:10-18

Colossians
3:5-6
3:23-24

11. Listed here are all the passages I have taken to have direct and specific relevance to the issue of wealth and possessions. Not all of them are cited (indeed, most of the texts from Luke are not), but intentionally all are taken into account in the constructive proposals to follow.

Conversely, not all of the texts referred to in the exposition of the canon are listed here. For example, the multiple commands to "love one another" from the Johannine texts are discussed above as part of the background for interpreting I John 3:17-18, but they are not listed because they are too general for our immediate purposes.

I Thessalonians
4:11
5:14

II Thessalonians
3:4

I Timothy
3:1-3
5:8
6:6-10
6:17-19

II Timothy
3:2

Titus
2:9-10
3:1

Hebrews
10:34
13:2-3, 5
13:16

James
1:9-11
2:1-9
2:15-16
4:1-10
5:1-6

I Peter
2:1
3:3-4
4:9
5:2

II Peter
2:3, 14

I John
3:17-21

III John
vv. 5-8

Jude
v. 11

The Apocalypse
2:9
3:14-19
13:16-17
18:3, 11-17
21:9-21

CHAPTER 8

Themes in the New Testament's Treatment of Wealth

AT THE CLOSE OF PART I, I laid out five methodological principles for using the New Testament to do normative ethics. The most general of them merely points out the necessary connection between methodology and exegesis;[1] it underlies this entire project in conception as well as execution. Two of the other principles call for attention to the implicit and explicit "moral world" in which instruction is given and makes sense[2] and to the particular rationale supporting specific moral injunctions.[3] These pertain in the first instance to the interpretation of individual passages. Attention to these literary and conceptual contexts is to be looked for in Part II, in the exegeses of individual texts, and in the remarks about the moral use of those texts in the contemporary church.

Now, however, I want to suggest that this same kind of appeal to the context and the function of moral instruction will help in applying the two remaining principles. These are the requirements that one take account of the entire New Testament canon[4] and of the differences within it,[5] and they pertain to the business of drawing conclusions about the overall moral witness of the New Testament on a particular topic.

The problem of dealing with the breadth and the diversity of the

1. See p. 36.
2. See p. 35.
3. See p. 33.
4. See p. 33.
5. See p. 33.

New Testament canon will take its shape from the kinds of diversity actually encountered there, on the one hand, and from the kind of moral use to which we seek to put these texts, on the other. (This is one of the ways in which methodology and exegesis are intertwined.) For example, to an interpreter who finds in Luke 12:33 ("Sell your possessions and give to the poor") a moral rule requiring complete divestiture, binding on all believers in every time and place, the equally clear injunction "Do not neglect hospitality" (Heb. 13:2) presents a problem. How can Christians invite strangers into their homes if they are not to own anything? Conversely, the interpreter who assumes that all such specific directives are morally irrelevant for the modern church has no such difficulty; however, she also has no moral guidance from the texts in question.

I have argued for a third option, one that looks for the rationale and the function of specific directives as these appear within the text as clues to their significance and to their continued appropriation. The point I wish to stress here is that this way of reading provides new resources for understanding and relating ethical material from disparate sources, as well as a means of making sense of the surprising variety sometimes encountered within single sources (e.g., the body of Lucan material on possessions). It is part of the task of exegesis to go beyond the explicit injunction or the single narrative to the argument that supports it and the purposes it is offered to serve, and these judgments can do more than control the ethical use of individual passages. They can inform the organization of specific texts into general categories that highlight the various kinds of moral significance wealth and possessions have within the New Testament canon. These categories in turn can shape contemporary ethical reflection by clarifying the kinds of questions to which the New Testament is suited to offer answers.

Obviously these generalizations about the moral meaning of wealth in the New Testament are only as good as the reading that underlies them, and they are always subject to critique and correction by the canon they seek to interpret. The goal of generalization and synthesis is to focus and illuminate this canon for our use. It is a necessary step if the church is ever to use the New Testament to form and inform its moral life and thought. But the test of its success is whether, when we return to the particular texts, as we must always do, we find that our sensibilities have been sharpened or blunted by our search for ordering principles. Given a topic like ours, which is addressed in some fashion in most of the books of the New Testament, it is not practicable actually to lay out the exegesis of every relevant passage. Nonetheless, the normative conclusions I will offer in this third part presuppose a careful reading of all the texts that have any relevance, and they stand open to any challenge that might arise from such a reading.

The Antecedent Tradition

We have seen in the exegesis of James 5:1-6 the extent to which the Jewish scriptural and intertestamental tradition about wealth can be presupposed or directly drawn upon in particular New Testament texts. Even when such materials are not cited or alluded to, however, they form part of the assumed moral and conceptual world for most of the New Testament. Jesus and his followers and later interpreters were for the most part heirs of this tradition, which formed their thinking partly as precedent and partly as counterpoint; it is clear that the New Testament material on wealth and possessions cannot completely be understood apart from it. Moreover, it is illuminating to see what of the tradition was carried forward directly, what was modified, and what was largely left behind. I will summarize the contributions of the Hebrew scriptures and apocrypha under four headings.[6]

Wealth as an Occasion for Idolatry

The first heading is idolatry: that is, material wealth in the Old Testament is repeatedly associated with apostasy, as the comforts of prosperity lead the people to rely on their wealth or, more commonly, on the adopted gods of their pagan neighbors as the source of their safety and their well-being. Thus, in Deuteronomy Israel is addressed as an animal that has become fat and sleek with the abundance God has provided, and has become rebellious and idolatrous, "forgetting the God who gave you birth" (Deut. 32:10-18). We find the prophets inveighing against those who have taken God's gifts and attributed them to the Baals or offered them in sacrifice to idols (Is. 2:6-8; Jer. 5:7; Ez. 16:15-22; Hosea 2:5-9). The

6. As indicated, citations throughout are exemplary and not exhaustive.

complacency and idleness of the wealthy are vividly depicted in Amos (6:4-7), where "those who lie upon beds of ivory" and "anoint themselves with the finest oils" "shall be the first to go into exile." Isaiah 3:16-24 condemns the luxury and pride of the daughters of Zion and prophesies their downfall; and Ezekiel foretells the loss of the gold and silver that Israel used to make idols: "They will throw their silver into the streets, and their gold will be an unclean thing . . . for it has made them stumble into sin" (Ez. 7:19-20). It would be easy to multiply citations, but these will suffice to illustrate the point. The effect is to cast rather a pall of suspicion on wealth as at least an occasion, if not the cause, of unfaithfulness to God.

Wealth as the Fruit of Injustice

The next strand of the tradition is also suspicious of wealth, but for a different reason. Here the issue is not the spiritual corruption wealth may bring in its train, but the injustice and lack of charity that is often the occasion of its accumulation. In this body of texts, if anything more plentiful than the last, wealth is associated with fraud, corruption of the judicial process, and neglect of the laws instituted by God to prevent the means of wealth from being concentrated in the hands of a few. In the prophets from Isaiah to Malachi, the accusation is that the rich have become so by using false dealing and dishonest weights and measures (e.g., Mic. 6:10-12) and by taking advantage of the poor, especially widows and orphans who are without any protection (e.g., Is. 10:1-3).

The language of these indictments is fierce and colorful. The wealthy are accused: "The plunder of the poor is in your houses. What do you mean by grinding the faces of the poor?" (Is. 3:14-15). Isaiah declares woe upon those who deprive the poor of their rights: "Where will you leave your riches" he asks, "when disaster comes?" (10:1-3). Jeremiah declares, "they are all greedy for unjust gain," and says that it is because they are "full of treachery," that they grow great and rich (5:27-28). Since they "sell the righteous for silver," "oppress the poor and crush the needy," declares Amos (2:6, 4:1) they will be "dragged into exile with fishhooks" (Amos 4:2).

And not only violence and oppression are condemned: the provisions of the covenant requiring the forgiveness of debts, the return of alienated land to the impoverished in the jubilee year, and the freeing of those sold into slavery are also binding, and to violate them is to invite God's wrath. Zechariah recounts the punishment that was visited upon Jerusalem because it refused to hear God's word requiring mercy and compassion for the defenseless poor: "Because they made their hearts as hard as flint . . . I scattered them with a whirlwind among the nations. The land was left desolate behind them" (7:14).

Wealth as the Blessing on the Faithful

But the witness of the Old Testament is no more univocal than that of the New; material wealth and prosperity are not by any means associated only with unfaithfulness and injustice. The same Deuteronomic and prophetic traditions that excoriate the apostasy, oppression, and heartlessness of the rich promise all manner of abundance as the consequence of fidelity to God and God's covenant. There is no trace of irony as both the law and the prophets depict the overflowing of grain and wine and oil, the proliferation of flocks and herds, and even the flow of golden tribute from vassal states that will be the result of faithfulness (Lev. 26:3-5, 9-10; Deut. 11:13-15; Is. 54:11-12; 60:9-16; Jer. 33:6-9; etc.). All these are to be part of God's fulfillment of the promise to the patriarchs to bring them to "a land flowing with milk and honey" (Ex. 3:8). God's sending material abundance is part and parcel of the "life" that the Israelites are called upon to choose when they ratify the Deuteronomic covenant, part of the comprehensive providence of the Lord, to whom belongs the earth and everything in it. Thus the great prophetic promises of restoration that climax Isaiah, Jeremiah, Ezekiel, and the minor prophets all include visions of future abundance, as a reordered sacral life is reflected in the peace and plenty of the temporal order.

Accordingly, the wisdom traditions can view individual prosperity as a mark of God's favor and its withdrawal as a sign of his judgment.[7]

7. They are not by any means consistent in this respect. "Ruthless men gain only wealth" (11:16) is also a proverb, and the same chapter that promises "the Lord does not let the righteous go hungry, but thwarts the cravings of the wicked" (Pr. 10:3) can speak of "ill-gotten riches" (Pr. 10:2). The point to be made is only that both traditions are present within the canon.

"The man that fears the Lord," promises Psalm 25, "will spend his days in prosperity, and his descendants will inherit the land" (v. 13). By contrast, the wealth of the wicked is short-lived; they will "soon wither like the grass" (Ps. 37:2). Whereas the inheritance of the blameless will endure (37:18), "in days of famine . . . the wicked will perish" (37:20). "Never have I seen [the righteous man's] children begging bread" (37:25), avows the psalmist, but "the offspring of the wicked will be cut off" (37:28). "The blessing of the Lord brings wealth," asserts Proverbs flatly (10:22), and "prosperity is the reward of the righteous" (13:21), but "poverty pursues the sinner" (Pr. 13:21; cf. 13:25).

Wealth as the Reward of Labor

The fourth and final heading under which the view of wealth in the Old Testament and Apocrypha can be summarized might be called "worldly prudence." It regards material prosperity as the result of the care and diligence of the rich, and conversely treats poverty as a sign of the idleness and profligacy of the poor. This strand of the tradition is limited to the wisdom materials of Proverbs and the apocryphal book of Sirach. This tradition reflects an understanding of spiritual wisdom as allied with practical sagacity and discretion, and places these words in the mouth of the figure of Wisdom: "With me are riches and honor, enduring wealth and prosperity. . . . I [bestow] wealth on those who love me" (Pr. 8:18, 21). Hard work, thrift, and discipline bring prosperity as their well-deserved fruit (Pr. 10:4; 12:11, 24; 13:4; 14:23; 21:5), but laziness, waste, and self-indulgence are responsible for poverty and want (20:4, 13; 21:17, 20; 23:5, 21). Proverbs 10:4 is typical: "A slack hand causes poverty, but the hand of the diligent makes rich."

This, then, is the framework of ideas about the moral and spiritual status of wealth into which the early church was born and in which its reflection and revisioning took place. The first two themes (wealth as a temptation to idolatry and as a symptom of injustice) come forward more or less directly into New Testament treatments of the topic (although typically they are given a distinctive "spin" by the Christian writers who employ them). The third theme, that of wealth as a medium and reflection of God's blessing on the righteous, comes through only in a much-tempered form: as an exhortation to gratitude for material needs being met, or as a promise of resources provided for the purpose of being given away.[8] At the same time, its fundamental affirmation of the material world as a good gift of God forms one pole of the New Testament witness. The fourth theme, that of wealth as the sign and fruit of the diligence and shrewdness of the wealthy, drops out of sight almost completely; a trace of its attitude toward work may be seen in the demand found in certain of the Pauline and pastoral epistles that Christians earn their own livelihoods by honest labor.

Themes in the New Testament's Treatment of Wealth

As I go on from here to develop what I take to be the broad themes and central concerns that shape the New Testament material on wealth and possessions, I will not attempt to be exhaustive, or to fit every text into one of the categories I outline. These are only the broad strokes on a canvas with considerable detail, intended to highlight what seem to me major, consistent, and repeated themes — ways of looking at the issues and problems raised by ownership that are important within the canon. They often have more to do with the reasons for which particular injunctions are given and the arguments with which they are supported than with the specifics of the injunctions themselves. Still, once again these categories are drawn from the particular texts, all of which must be taken into account.

Wealth as a Stumbling Block

The first kind of moral significance ascribed to wealth in the New Testament is that found in the passage from Mark we examined in Chapter 3: wealth is accounted an obstacle to discipleship, a practical hindrance to those who would follow Jesus. The story of the one who found he could not sell his possessions to follow Jesus and find eternal life, whose parallel we noted in Matthew 19:16ff., appears as well in Luke 18:18-30. Each time it is accompanied by the word of Jesus declaring the human impossibility of the rich entering the kingdom of God. As I noted earlier,[9] taken

8. Cf. II Cor. 9:11.
9. See above, p. 45.

together these passages provide the only example in scripture of an individual being called to follow Jesus and clearly refusing.[10] This same idea of wealth as a hindrance to hearing and heeding the gospel is contained in the interpretation of the parable of the sower, likewise found in all three synoptic gospels (Mt. 13:22, Mk. 4:18-19, Lk. 8:14). There the "deceitfulness of wealth" (Matthew) or "the desire for other things" (Mark) or "the riches and pleasures of the world" (Luke) choke the implanted word, so that even though the gospel is heard, it never comes to fruition. Conversely, the picture given of the ones who *do* respond to Jesus' preaching of the kingdom is predominantly (though, it is important to note, not *exclusively*)[11] a picture of those who have "left everything and followed him" (Lk. 5:11, 28; cf. Mk. 1:16-17, Mt. 4:18-22, and Jn. 1:37-39). It is to these who have met the demand for dispossession that Jesus promises treasure in heaven and eternal life, as well as a hundredfold recompense "with persecutions, now in this life" (Mk. 10:31 and par.). Similarly, the disciples who are sent out to preach are instructed to go without supplies and rely on hospitality for their livelihood (Mt. 10:8-10; Lk. 9:1-3, 10:4, 7). It is to them that Jesus says "rejoice that your names are enrolled in heaven" (Lk. 10:20).

However, though poverty may characterize the disciples, it does not define discipleship, nor is it even central to it. As I tried to make clear in the treatment of Mark 10:17-31, the importance of possessions (or their lack) in these texts is entirely derivative and instrumental. The concern in all the passages cited here is that the good news be heard and received and proclaimed in turn; poverty when it is called for is merely a condition of liberty for hearing and proclaiming the gospel. In the gospels, the concern

10. Cf. Mt. 8:20-22 and especially Lk. 10:57-62. In neither of these passages is it expressly stated whether the would-be disciples do in fact follow or not. It is also interesting to note the connections between these texts and Mk. 10:28-30 and par. They warn of homelessness as the price of discipleship, and of the conflict between familial obligations and following Christ. If, as usually interpreted, the request to "bury my father" is really a request to wait until the father has died and the son received his inheritance, this too may be a concern for financial security.

11. The most detailed picture is offered in Luke/Acts, where women disciples are said to have "provided for [Jesus] out of their means" (Lk. 7:19ff.), where Jesus can speak of believers giving a feast and inviting the poor (Lk. 14:12ff.), and where churches meet in the homes of believers. Figures like Zaccheus (Lk. 19:1-10) and Mary and Martha (Lk. 10:38ff.) also belie the idea that all who are accounted followers of Jesus are itinerant and propertyless.

for material wealth repeatedly thwarts the response to Jesus' preaching, and thus it takes on centrality as the occasion for that failure. But even then the point is the inability to respond, the paralysis of being tied to the things one owns. In that sense it does not matter whether one's possessions are sold or not — all that matters is whether one follows.

Wealth as a Competing Object of Devotion

The second theme in the New Testament's treatment of wealth and possessions is already familiar from our review of the Old Testament: possessions and the love of them stand as a continual temptation to idolatry, not in the form of Baal worship but in the rather more modern form of taking wealth itself as the primary object of love, trust, and attachment. This is the concern encountered in the Lucan passage we examined in Chapter 4, that material wealth constantly tempts its possessors to find in it an alternative ground of security and self-definition. Pointedly the gospels warn, "You cannot serve God and mammon" (Mt. 6:24, Lk. 16:13), and the disciples are counseled not to accumulate treasures on earth (Mt. 6:19) because their hearts will inevitably follow (Mt. 6:21, Lk. 12:31). They are particularly cautioned against the delusion that possessions can provide safety: "Be on guard against every kind of greed, for no one's life consists in the abundance of things he has" (Lk. 12:15). This is the occasion of the parable of the rich farmer (Lk. 12:16-21), and it is noteworthy that the man who relies on his wealth for security and rest is called not wicked but a fool, because he has placed his trust in what cannot save him (cf. I Tim. 6:17-19).

Repeatedly in the epistles greed is bluntly equated with idolatry (Eph. 4:28, Col. 3:6), and believers are warned in the letters to Timothy and the Hebrews to keep themselves free of the love of money, a sin for which the wrath of God is coming upon the earth (I Tim. 6:6-8, II Tim. 3:2, Heb. 13:5). The rich particularly are cautioned not to "set their hopes on riches" (I Tim. 6:17-19), and that same letter goes so far as to call the love of money "a root of all evils" and a snare that has led some away from faith in God (I Tim. 6:10). James warns against the lust for worldly things as a kind of infidelity, appropriating Isaiah's figure of adultery for those who transfer the devotion that should be God's to other objects (4:1-10).

Inseparable from these warnings against the peril of ownership and the potential for idolatry is the positive purpose for which even the most radical injunctions to complete dispossession are offered — for they never come in isolation. The point is not to avoid having treasures on earth, but rather to secure them in heaven, "where rust cannot corrupt nor thief steal." From the perspective of the New Testament, it makes no difference whether anyone serves mammon or not, unless he in fact serves God instead. Similarly, there is no use in a person not being anxious about her life if all she achieves is a stoic indifference to the contingencies of this world; all that matters is whether she is free to love and seek God's kingdom and righteousness.

Thus, from the standpoint of the gospels where the most radical injunctions to abandon property are found, in one sense it is giving too much importance to material possessions to look for a consistent rule about what one may own or how one ought to meet the basic needs for food, clothing, and shelter. A genuinely openhearted generosity may be as real a response to welcoming God's kingdom as voluntary poverty; therefore Zaccheus's fourfold restitution for fraud and his offer of half his goods to the poor can be greeted with the pronouncement, "Today salvation has come to this house!" (Lk. 19:10). If the first and second themes of the New Testament on wealth are that possessions tend to hinder discipleship and that all riches tempt one to trust in them rather than in God, then there is a corollary to both of these. Poverty is not to be sought for itself, or as a guarantor of moral purity, but only as a means of securing the liberty for undivided obedience and loyalty to God's reign. Within the view of reality advocated in the New Testament, literally nothing else matters.

Under the broad heading of this liberty we may place all the injunctions to give alms to all who ask for them (Mt. 5:42 and par.), to lend without expecting return (Lk. 6:35, cf. Mt. 5:42), and to offer our cloak to the one who takes our tunic (Mt. 5:40 and par.), as well as the multiple instructions to ask confidently for whatever we need, with no doubting. For examples of such liberty we may cite all those who hold possessions in common (Acts 2:44-45, 4:32-37), or who make them available for the support of the church and its ministers (Lk. 8:2-3, Phil. 4:10-18), or who place them as offerings without reserve to meet the needs of others (Mk. 12:41-44 and par., II Cor. 8:1-4). Here too we can locate the peculiar-sounding advice of Paul that those who buy and sell behave as if they had no goods (I Cor. 7:30). Possessions of themselves will no more bar admission to the kingdom than poverty of itself will secure it; as it is possible "to give up everything one owns" and yet "have no charity" (I Cor. 13:3), it is possible ("with God") for even the rich to enter the kingdom. In short, poverty in the New Testament is not an ideal but only a tool. But lest the affluent be comforted too soon, in the gospels at least it is a tool few can do without.

Wealth as a Symptom of Economic Injustice

The third theme is, like the second, carried over from the Hebrew Scriptures and Apocrypha: the association of wealth with evil and oppression, and of the poor with those who await God's vindication. This is clearest in Luke's gospel, where the announcement of the gospel is portrayed as bringing blessing to the poor and woe to the rich (1:51-53, 4:18-19, 6:21, 16:19-26, etc.). A similar assessment of wealth is evident in the Apocalypse. There the whore of Babylon and those who profit from her vices are depicted as wealthy and over-indulged (e.g., 17:3-4, 18:9-19), while the faithful churches and the martyrs under the throne are poor (2:8-10, 7:16-17), and those who refuse the "mark of the beast" are the victims of economic oppression (13:16-17). As we have seen, this theme is also found strikingly in the epistle of James.

We have noted James's attack on preferential treament for the wealthy, in which he asks rhetorically, "Is it not the rich who oppress you?" (2:5). The epistle also includes an analysis of sin, which presents greed as the source of strife and murder (4:1-2). The excoriation of the abuses of the wealthy that he goes on to deliver in 5:1-6 is every bit as scathing as anything found in the prophets, and brings out an important point about the substance of the New Testament indictment of the rich. Along with the accusations of fraudulent labor practices and corruption of the judicial process that James treats as species of murder, the epistle condemns the wealthy for failing to give alms out of their accumulated wealth (5:2-3) and for indulging in luxuries while others are in want (5:5).

As in Luke's parable of the rich man and Lazarus (16:19-26) and Matthew's parable of the sheep and the goats (25:31-46), the "testimony against you" that threatens the rich in James 5:2-3 is simply for failing to give help. Nothing in these texts suggests that those so indicted are causally responsible for the needs they ignore. Simply failing to share one's possessions with the needy is culpable, a defiance of God's demand for love and charity toward the neighbor. Together these passages make clear that judgment is not reserved solely for those who actively rob and exploit the poor or use their wealth for corruption. Unjust distribution is condemned along with unjust accrual and unjust use.

Wealth as a Resource for Human Needs

The final major theme of the New Testament regarding possessions is that ownership carries concrete and wide-ranging responsibilities. Most notably, the material support of fellow believers is a natural and necessary expression of the love and unity that bind the body of Christ. We have seen that the epistles of John in particular treat love of the sisters and brothers as a sure test of love for God, and challenge the reality of any professed love that does not share the means of bodily life with those in need (I John 3:16-17; cf. James 2:15-16). In the description of the Jerusalem community in Acts, such sharing is the earmark of the fellowship of the saved (2:44-47) and a token that the believers are "one in heart and mind" (4:32-35).

We also found the expectation of economic sharing with other Christians characteristic of Paul. Tangible resources are one of the gifts that exist for the good of the whole community (Rom. 12:6-8). Therefore, not only are the infant churches to share all things with those who teach them the gospel (Gal. 6:6), and generally contribute to the needs of the saints (Rom. 12:13), but three of Paul's extant letters exhort the liberal contribution of Gentile churches to the relief of the church in Jerusalem (Rom. 15:25-27, I Cor. 16:1-2, II Cor. 8–9). Moreover, as we saw in Chapter 5, in the two full chapters of II Corinthians that he devotes to this matter, Paul assumes that the aim of giving between Christian communities is to be the equal meeting of the needs of all. As we noted there,[12] he is careful to assert that he asks rather than commands the Corinthians' gifts; nonetheless, he concludes, "through the test (δοκιμῆς) of this ministry you will glorify God by your obedience to your confession of the gospel" (II Cor. 9:13). Such a formulation identifies this material service to fellow believers as a matter of obedience, a proof or test of the truthfulness of the confession of Christ that saves them.

12. See p. 87.

All the texts we have examined in this section have dealt with responsibilities to those within the Christian community, and this is in fact the predominant subject addressed in the New Testament canon. However, there is also a canonical foundation for a universal duty to care for the needy. Beside the general admonition to "give to every one who asks you" (Mt. 5:42, Lk. 6:30), and the instruction to invite the poor in to feast (Lk. 14:12-14), there is the general command to love the neighbor (cited six times), which is explicitly extended to include the stranger and the enemy (Mt. 5:43-48; Lk. 6:27, 32-35). That this generalized love is to include concrete provision for material needs is implied by Jesus' own gloss on the command to neighbor love, the parable of the Good Samaritan (Lk. 10:29-37). It is also expressly stated by Paul when he commands "If your enemy is hungry, feed him" (Rom. 12:20).

In light of these teachings, the special obligation toward those within the Christian community is to be interpreted as an addition to, rather than a restriction of, the requirements of neighbor love generally. It is analogous to the special responsibility individuals are thought to have to provide for the needs of their own families. Paul summarizes the practical ethic that is to guide Christians: "so far as it is in your power, do good to all, and especially to those who are of the household of faith" (Gal. 6:10).

The Development of the Tradition

Finally, it is important to note what is missing from the canon as well as what is present. As noted above, those strands of the Old Testament tradition that treat wealth and prosperity as signs of God's favor toward the righteous, or as the fruit of the wisdom and diligence of the rich, have largely disappeared from view. Moreover, they have been replaced by the general expectation that faithfulness will entail hardship, including material want. Nonetheless, the Hebrew doctrines of creation and providence continue to make themselves felt.

If righteousness is not expected to bring riches, still believers are encouraged to rely on God for the provision of their basic needs, and both example (Acts 4:34) and instruction (Mt. 6:33, Lk. 6:31, II Cor. 9:10-11) affirm that God will give God's people what they need to sustain them in their obedient life. And while material wealth may no longer be attributed to the virtues of the rich or taken as a sign of God's approval, neither is it attributed to the devil. There is in the New Testament no pure asceticism that deprecates material reality as intrinsically evil, and no talk of a mystical ascent to God by means of a withdrawal from bodily reality.

The dangers of distraction and entanglement, of misplaced trust and loyalty that inhere in ownership are all brought forward, but there is no repudiation of material goods as such. The disciples may be directed to sell their possessions and give them to the poor; they are never directed simply to throw them away. The necessity and goodness of wealth as a resource for the meeting of human needs are affirmed; and as we have seen, the same epistles that condemn greed as idolatrous can command provision for oneself and one's family as a duty. Even in the Apocalypse, despite the attack on the luxury of the wicked, the writer sees no impropriety in depicting the excellences of the New Jerusalem in terms of material richness, wealth, and beauty. The City of God has streets of pure gold and walls set with jewels.

Instead of antimaterialism or a generalized "hostility to wealth,"[13] we find specific theological and moral rationales for the attitude toward material possessions in the writings of the New Testament. Material wealth is problematic because it is often a hindrance to heeding the gospel; it is dangerous because it is a temptation to the sin of idolatry; it is suspect because it is frequently the result or the means of social injustice; finally, its disposition is a matter of great moral weight, as the response to human needs is a sign of the advent of God's kingdom and a test of the love that identifies Jesus' true followers. With these themes and principles in hand, we are finally in a position to return to the issue with which we began this inquiry: the way in which the New Testament can guide and inform the church's moral discernment regarding wealth and possessions.

13. The phrase is Thomas Schmidt's in his book, *Hostility to Wealth in the Synoptic Gospels* (Sheffield: JSOT Press, 1987).

CHAPTER 9

The New Testament on the Moral Status of Wealth: Learning to Ask the Canon's Questions

The New Testament as a Tool for Moral Discernment

I HAVE DEVOTED a great deal of the preceding six chapters to trying to understand not only what things the New Testament says about wealth and possessions, but why it says them. In the exegesis of individual passages, this has led me to examine the arguments advanced for particular admonitions within the text and to consider the context and function of each passage within the larger body of the gospel or epistle of which it is part and within the implicit social and conceptual world in which it operated. In the summary review of the canon, I have given attention to the whole body of material on wealth found in a given source and to how it relates to the writer's or redactor's broader theological concerns.

In the preceding chapter, I used the reasons advanced (whether implicitly or explicitly) for the moral teaching on wealth in various texts as the basis for organizing passages into thematic groups, reflecting different kinds of moral concern about possessions. This exercise serves a number of purposes. First, as I stated at the outset,[1] it helps to order and focus a large and diverse body of injunctions, prohibitions, exhortations, and narratives, making them more available for our consideration. Further, by lifting up the common concerns that underlie the diversity of the New Testament canon, it

1. See above, p. 122.

helps us to understand the tensions within it, and sometimes even to reconcile directives that are, on the face of it, inconsistent.

Perhaps most important, this strategy provides us with a way to obtain useful guidance from the concrete injunctions of the New Testament even when the enormous cultural and economic changes of twenty centuries, and the markedly different situation of the church after two thousand years of its life, make it impossible or undesirable for modern congregations to appropriate them directly. To use the language established in Part I, it provides us with a tool for raising the "level of moral discourse" from concrete rules to more general principles, ideals, and goals when this is called for.

It should be noted that the methodological principle that gives prima facie weight to specific moral rules and concrete directives is still in force. I see no reason to suppose, for example, that the "rule" requiring that those selected as church leaders not be greedy (I Tim. 3:3) is any less applicable now than in the first century. But we have seen that the New Testament simply will not provide consistent, generalizable moral rules about what one may own or how one is obliged to provide for necessary food, shelter, and clothing. However, even when it *is* necessary to resort to a higher level of discourse because of the diversity or situational specificity of the canon's imperatives, the contribution of the New Testament is not limited to principles so general that they are entirely vague and innocuous. An example will serve to illustrate the point.

If (as I have argued in Chapter 4) the point of the Lucan discourse about anxiety and possessions (12:22-34) is to draw out the implications of Jesus' advent for economic life, then there is a third option, which is neither to disregard it nor to take its call for divestiture as a permanent and binding rule. Instead, it may serve the church as a call to single-heartedness and a warning against the insidious idolatry of a safety mediated by what one owns. Within this framework, its imperative "Sell your possessions and give them to the poor" stands as a model of, and a provocation to, "seeking first God's kingdom." It is a counterweight to *every* complacent self-assurance, "I have given enough," and a continual challenge to consider what the church's material life says about the true objects of its trust and its worship. To take it seriously *as* a model is to call into question many of the assumptions of middle-class existence, including the fundamental assumption that there *is* such a thing as "economic security" and that Christians are entitled to it.

Depending on what sort of ethical guidance one is looking for, moral instruction of this form may be a disappointment. Certainly it will be if the church is looking for a rule to follow, either in the ordinary sense of a law to abide by or in the rather more interesting sense of a clearly and comprehensively ordered way of life: for example, the Rule of St. Benedict. However, we have already acknowledged that both the cultural and economic context of the church's life and the position of the church within that context have been altered beyond recognition by the intervening centuries. Recognizing the practical differences created by the two thousand years that separate us from the original writers and readers of these texts, we are forced to conclude that neither of these forms of "rule" would be of much use to us in any case. But if the normative result of our study of the New Testament material on wealth is not to take the form of concrete rules, or even ethical principles with a clear and fixed application, what form can it take? I suggest that it most naturally takes the form of *questions:* questions that the New Testament, as the central and privileged text of the Christian community, puts to those who acknowledge its moral authority.

These are not simple questions, ones that can be answered "yes" or "no" and dispensed with. They are questions intended for the ongoing examination of the community's life. They serve to reframe our twentieth-century inquiries about the ethics of property into the form in which the New Testament is prepared to entertain them, the form in which their theological significance is clear and central. The questions are here organized into categories that correspond to the major themes in the New Testament's treatment of possessions as I developed them in the preceding chapter. They are, as it were, addressed to the Christian community by the texts it calls "Scripture," and they express the issues raised by wealth and possessions as these are understood across the New Testament canon. The questions are offered as tools for use in the moral and practical discernment of contemporary Christian bodies regarding issues of property. Accordingly, they are framed in the first person plural, as it is only thus, in the self-examination and self-criticism of a gathered community, that they can legitimately be appealed to as norms. More will be said later about what must characterize such bodies for these questions to be useful and illuminating and for the process of collective discernment to be of any practical import. Finally, each category ends with a "hook," a "test case" in the form of a scriptural text that poses the central question in that category as pointedly as possible.

Asking the Questions

Questions About Liberty

The first set of questions expresses the New Testament's theme of wealth as a stumbling block, a hindrance to responding to the call to discipleship.

Q Do we as members of contemporary congregations find ourselves at liberty to hear God's call to us, whatever it is, or are we too encumbered by the things we own — or the things we desire?

Q Are we aware of the ways in which increasing numbers of possessions bind us more and more closely to a particular location, a particular set of tasks, a particular level of income — in short, to a particular life?

Q Can we be confident of our ability to discern a vocation in the midst of the competing pressures simply to sustain the kind of material lifestyle we have attained? Is there anything for which we would literally give all that we owned? What would have to be at stake?

Q Could we hear a call that asked us to leave it all behind? How do we know?

The question of whether any particular individual or group is in fact being called upon to leave any or all possessions behind always remains. It remains because the point and purpose of "evangelical poverty" is evangelism (broadly construed), or more precisely the liberty for it; and it is formally possible to possess even great wealth without being bound to it or constrained by it. But the attention given across the canon to wealth as a particular hazard ought to make an interpreter wary of treating it as simply one among many possible obstacles.

Just as it is entirely possible to consume alcohol, even quite regularly, without being "bound to it or constrained by it," it is possible also to be *utterly* bound by it, and we rightly suspect the liberty of those who say too often, "Oh, I could stop drinking any time — if I wanted to." In the case of those who repeat that same line in the face of evidence that their consumption is doing harm to them or to someone else, our suspicion hardens into certainty that what we confront is not the liberty of conscience, but the bondage of addiction. Perhaps addiction is the most illuminating contemporary analogy for the problem posed by possessions; only the demonstrable ability to stop "consuming" any time our own or others' needs require it can prove the liberty that makes consumption morally harmless. In short, the only way one can be certain that possessions do not represent a moral and spiritual peril is continually to leave them behind!

The test case for this category is the declaration of Mark 10:25 and its parallels: "It is easier for a camel to go through the eye of a needle than for the rich to enter the Kingdom of God." Coupled with Jesus' observation, "for men it is impossible," this poses as acutely as anything may the *human* impossibility of possessing without being in the power of what is possessed, and it is a blunt reminder of what the gospels suppose to be at stake.

Questions About Worship

This second group of questions is occasioned by the large body of New Testament texts that view wealth and possessions as temptations to idolatry, occasions to find one's identity, interests, and ultimate safety in something other than God.

Q What do we in the modern church trust, and where do we look for our security? What do we rely upon for our protection, and what do we protect in turn? How do accumulated wealth or other vehicles of "financial security" figure in our estimates of our own safety?

Q What do we hope for most in our lives? Conversely, what do we fear most deeply? How are these things bound up with the level of our material existence?

Q How do contemporary Christians define themselves? By occupation, or social class, or familial status? What are the standards by which we measure the success or failure of our lives? In the realm of material possessions, how do we decide how much is "enough"?

Q What do we pursue above everything else? On what basis do we make decisions about where we work, where we live, and what we do with our time? What do these decisions reveal about the central values of our lives, and how do they contribute to reinforcing them?

Q What is the crucial object of loyalty for modern believers, that for the sake of which we live the lives we have chosen for ourselves? If we claim that God is the central loyalty in our lives, what evidence exists for the truth of that claim in the material lives we lead?

Again, these questions have no answers built in; no specific and inevitable judgment is implied about what Christians ought to own, or what sort of work they ought to do, or what kind of material "lifestyle" is compatible with Christian faith. Taken together, they are intended to explore the relationship between what those who profess Christianity own and what they conceive of as the source and the end of their existence. They are an invitation to look at the role of possessions in self-understanding and in the shaping of the practical choices a person makes. Indirectly, they reflect the gospels' assumptions that what one does is inseparable from what one believes and that what one serves is the only reliable indication of what one loves.

The test case for this category is the flat statement of Matthew 6:24, found also in Luke 16:13: "You cannot serve God and mammon." Implicit in this declaration is the idea that every human life is in service to something, and that the goal that governs human choices and orders human lives is in actual fact the object of worship, whatever it may be called. It forces on us the awareness that possessions continually compete for the devotion of Christian believers and challenge their obedience to the first commandment, which demands "You shall have no other gods before me."

Questions About Justice

The third group of questions for moral discernment corresponds to the New Testament's treatment of wealth as frequently the product and the means of oppression. The questions address three areas of economic justice: the accrual of wealth, its use, and its distribution.

Q To what extent is the wealth of modern Christians the product of injustice in the form of coercive or exploitative practices in labor, management, or marketing?

Q To what extent does our material prosperity rest upon and help to perpetuate unjust structures and institutions?

Q Can we defend the work we do in terms of its contribution to human good and its compatibility with Christian obligations to love and serve the neighbor?

Q How do contemporary Christians make use of the social power conferred by wealth? Are our economic resources used to give unfair access to, or privileged treatment within, the mechanisms of law and government? To coerce the behavior of others?

Q Do we hold idle assets that might be used to help those in dire need? Can we defend our share of the benefits and burdens of society as just and equitable?

Questions about justice in the accumulation, use, and distribution of wealth can also be addressed to the public institutions which Christians participate in and thereby help to support. Of particular concern in both Testaments is the potential of wealth for fostering corruption and inequity in the political and judicial structures of a society. Beyond the question of outright bribery, we face the issue of how wealth is related to the concentration or abuse of political power and influence and the problem of how the operation of the legal system differs for those with or without material assets. Because of the complexity and intractability of structural or systematic inequities in the socioeconomic mechanisms of a society, there will always be room for disagreement about the most effective and appropriate strategy for redressing such injustices. Nonetheless, the New Testament's concern for economic justice does provide criteria for judging public institutions and grounds for Christian engagement in efforts at systematic reform.

The test case for the questions about justice is the text from James 5:1: "Woe to you rich! Begin to weep and cry out for the miseries which are coming upon you!" As we have seen,[2] in the verses that follow, James

2. See above, pp. 98-100.

draws upon Old Testament and apocryphal traditions to condemn the wealthy who hoard their goods and give nothing to the poor, who accumulate their wealth by cheating their laborers, and who use their power to corrupt the judicial process. The passage will stand for the condemnation of all kinds of economic injustices and for the retribution of the Lord of Hosts that is said to await them.

Questions About Care

The final category of questions for use in the moral discernment of Christian communities concerns the responsibilities that ownership entails. There is a special focus on meeting the needs of other Christians toward whom they bear a particular obligation as "members of the household of faith." However, the needs of all others also fall within the scope of New Testament injunctions as belonging to the category "neighbor," which is to include strangers and even enemies.

Q If the sign and test of discipleship is the love Christians have toward each other, can we support our claim to be disciples? Is the love we are commanded to have toward other Christians displayed in action, or merely professed in word?

Q Can we modern believers justify the present allocation of our material resources in light of the needs of those we call sisters and brothers? Does our response to the needs of other Christians reflect the unity and equality that are to characterize the body of Christ?

Q By what standard do we determine what we will keep and what we will give away? Is the motive and aim of our giving that all needs be met equally? How do we distinguish between our own needs and our desires?

Q Is the care of the modern church for the material needs of other human beings an imitation and a sign of God's love for all persons, even "the selfish and the ungrateful"?

Q Is our generosity toward others who have no "claim" on us a model and reflection of God's generosity in Christ?

Questions like these do not provide clear and specific standards for giving; they don't ask whether Christians meet requirements in dollar amounts or in percentages of income. But we have seen that the New Testament's calls for almsgiving and for economic sharing with other Christians have two foundations, each of which has clear implications for how much believers are to give. One of these is Christ's own self-gift, which can only be the basis of an uncalculating and sacrificial generosity. The other, based on the oneness of the body of Christ, exerts a strong pressure toward equality in distribution. Both of these appeals are present in the passage we examined from II Corinthians.

It can be argued that the historical and material context of these texts indicates that the equality envisioned was equality in subsistence, not a strict division of assets above and beyond those needed for basic health and welfare. There was in the first century no existing economy that provided substantial and widespread "disposable income"; certainly the modern situation, with the scale and complexity of its economic structures, and the array of its products, was not only unanticipated but unthinkable. It is reasonable to assume, for example, that the collection for Jerusalem was undertaken to meet basic needs, not to ensure strict equality of income.

But even with these caveats and restrictions, the consequences of adopting a goal like "equality in the meeting of needs" would be startling. A modest example from the setting of urban North America will illustrate the point. If the Christian congregations of the relatively affluent suburbs felt a moral obligation to share their resources with local inner city congregations only to the point where the latter had the basic needs of life (decent food, housing, and clothing) and access to the basic social goods (like education and health care), the lives of most congregations, rich and poor, would be unrecognizable.

The test case for questions about material care for others is provided by the challenge of I John: "If you have the means of worldly life and see your brother in need, yet close your heart to him, how does the love of God remain in you? Let your love not be in words on the tongue, but in action and in truth" (3:17). It serves to underline the impossibility of a love for God that does not result in practical care for the neighbor.

The Necessary Context of Discernment: Sharing a Moral World

The function of these questions in informing Christian moral reflection is twofold: First, by highlighting what the New Testament understands to be the moral importance of material possessions, they help to ensure that we inquire of its teachings in ways to which this canon is suited to respond. Second, these questions offer positive moral goals for the economic life of Christians, and they provide some genuine tests for compliance with New Testament norms regarding the treatment of wealth. Taken with any degree of seriousness, the ideas that possessions are quite likely to defeat the desire to follow Christ or that the natural norm for deciding what to keep and what to give away is that the needs of all in the community be met equally have the potential to remake the material lives of affluent modern Christians in a fundamental way.

Still, the fact remains that the moral goals of liberty for and loyalty to God's kingdom, and equity and generosity in the accrual and use of material wealth, cannot be translated into a single, universally applicable pattern of material life, or into a checklist of what may be owned and what must be given away. Moreover, the use of moral questions rather than moral rules or even ethical principles places a heavy reliance on the capacity for self-insight and self-criticism, and there is no proof against either self-delusion or hypocrisy. This is part of the reason for the specification that these questions are intended for use in the context of the moral reflection of particular Christian *communities:* their purpose is to guide the process of collective moral discernment in which Christians not only counsel one another but call one another to account.

This setting of discernment about wealth within the context of the ongoing life of actual communities respects the fact that economic life is an aspect of *social* existence. This means that wealth and poverty are always intrinsically relative judgments, conditioned by the historical circumstances of particular groups. Only in concrete and situated communities can general obligations be assessed in light of actual material conditions. Moreover, only within particular bodies of Christians can decisions be reached about the disposal of collective resources, and only there can judgments about the mission and goals of the congregation guide decisions about how these are to be translated into shared standards for the community's material life.

Finally, and perhaps most crucially, the "social" character of economic ethics is central because money (or its cultural equivalents) is a medium of human relationship. It is a means and an expression of the complexity of our existence, both over against and in dependence upon one another. To change one's mind about money is less to change a set of ideas than to adopt a new pattern of social life. It is to embrace a new way of being together, and a new way of ordering and assessing our lives. This can only be the activity of a group, especially when the pattern and understanding it adopts is not only distinct from, but substantially opposed to, the one advocated and assumed by the surrounding dominant culture. In such a situation, only the church as a gathered community can provide the moral and practical support necessary for its members to live out an ethic of property notably at odds with that of the surrounding society. This support includes practical help for those whose generosity has left them in material want, but even more centrally it is a matter of providing a context of intelligibility for decisions that would otherwise seem irrational. Such a context must be sustained by ongoing community activities of reflection and critique, of remembrance and hope.

The idea that moral reflection and moral re-formation about the status of possessions must take place in communities of discernment and mutual accountability entails a number of things about the nature of the groups that might find the New Testament's moral instruction usable. One is that it presupposes a high level of commitment to the shared life of the group. On the most practical level, this commitment is needed because any such process is necessarily long-term; it must be pursued consistently over time by a group of people who remain engaged with one another and with the (decidedly uncomfortable) task of reassessing and reordering their material existence. More deeply, commitment is required because any serious consideration of the spiritual perils of wealth will involve a degree of honesty and self-disclosure that can be sustained only in an atmosphere of genuine care and trust. This is not a subject for a two-week annual stewardship campaign or the instant intimacy of a weekend retreat; the courage to achieve honesty must be developed, and the right to expect it must be earned. Finally, holding one another accountable to a moral tradition is hard work, requiring both humility and stubbornness, both patience and daring. To undertake it requires a high stake in the vitality and fidelity of the community's enactment of Christian faith.

But in order to perform all these functions, communities must also exhibit a high degree of agreement about the fundamental beliefs and practices that form the basis of their life together. Members of the community must be able to reach some unanimity about the general shape of Christian life and about the convictions and affirmations that are indispensable to their faith. They must have in common a basic understanding of the nature of the church and a broadly similar understanding of the role of Scripture within it.

These theological agreements are necessary because of the nature of the canon's teaching about possessions and because of the inseparability of that teaching from the cosmological, historical, and ecclesiological assumptions that make it intelligible. In short, in order to form a community of moral discourse capable of engaging in collective discernment and mutual admonition about the treatment of possessions, members of Christian bodies must share the context of ideas, stories, and assumptions that we have called a "moral world." Moreover, for the New Testament's attitudes and norms regarding wealth to retain their rationality and their practical force in the modern church, certain aspects of that contemporary "moral world" must be in continuity with the one in which the canon's texts were written and understood.

We have already discussed the necessity of this larger theological context in relation to individual passages, noting how the instrumental value of poverty in Mark requires some notion of a kingdom of God to be entered,[3] or how Paul's appeal to the generosity of Christ in exchanging his wealth for our poverty presupposes adherence to the story of Jesus' salvific death.[4] Now it is time to lay out in more comprehensive and systematic fashion the convictions, assumptions, stories, and expectations that undergird the New Testament's teaching on possessions, and explore what must be retained if these instructions and the questions they raise are to continue to form the moral life of the contemporary church. Finally, we will consider what becomes of these moral norms and attitudes regarding wealth and possessions where the beliefs that support them are repudiated, or simply allowed to atrophy.

Perhaps most notable, and in a sense most surprising, is the prominence of the eschatological horizon of Christian belief in forming the New Testament's ethic of property. This is in evidence not only in those (actually

3. See pp. 55-56.
4. See pp. 88-89.

rather few) texts where the imminence of the eschaton is assumed and used as a basis for disengagement from the ordinary business of buying and selling.[5] More often, it takes the form of an appeal to the greater significance of the kingdom as an object of desire and pursuit, or to the necessity of being "rich toward God" (Lk. 12:21), or to the greater value of the "imperishable inheritance" (I Peter 1:7) of God's grace, or to the futility of wealth as a refuge from divine judgment. Notably, none of these appeals is bound up with a conviction that the Parousia must be imminent in time. Nor do they require any particular understanding of the form that coming telos must take; in fact, there is room for a wide range of interpretations and for substantial differences in eschatology. These appeals do, however, require a positive belief in some kind of transcendent and transhistorical realm in which the poor are blessed and receive the inheritance of eternal life that is promised to those who forsake the security of material wealth for the sake of fidelity to the gospel.

This belief is necessary because, consistently, when the New Testament counsels people to abandon what they own, give their possessions as alms, be generous to their enemies, or cease defending their property rights, it is *in order that* they may do something else: find eternal life, have treasure in heaven, be the children of God, or enter the kingdom. Even the ringing condemnations of injustice are backed up by appeals to the judgment of God that will fall upon those who ignore or oppress the poor. The force of the appeals depends on the conviction of the truthfulness and reality of the consequences that are depicted because *they are fundamentally rational appeals.* These actions make sense because they serve what is held to be the ultimate value, the relationship with God, which is held to be eternal and immune from worldly contingencies. If the biblical language that depicts that relation is evacuated of all meaning, the force of the appeals disappears.

Also crucial for the force and intelligibility of the New Testament's moral teaching on wealth and possessions is belief in and adherence to the story of Jesus Christ, including the salvation accomplished by his death and resurrection. It is confidence in, and gratitude for, the "riches of salvation" that motivates and makes possible many of the economic attitudes and actions commanded in the New Testament. It is because of the "wealth of this glorious inheritance" that the fleeting treasures of the world

5. E.g., I Cor. 7:29, 31.

may be reckoned of no account, and because they know themselves to be gifted and graced by God in Christ that Christians may be commanded to imitate and extend God's generosity to brothers and enemies alike. Similarly, it is their conviction of Christ's ultimate victory over death that makes his acceptance of the vulnerability and humiliation of poverty a reasonable model for his followers. Without an active sense of this victory, and of the abundant resources it has made available, there is nothing to motivate the extraordinary generosity the New Testament calls for, and no "wealth" of grace to be shared.

Bound up with the centrality of the story of Jesus is the identification of the church as the community of primary loyalty. It is to supersede ties of kindred and culture, even the bonds to immediate family, as a locus of belonging and identity. In the writings of the New Testament, the community of followers is the crucial "reference group," joined together by what Jesus has done for all alike. This unity and equality is to be reflected in the sharing of possessions within the congregation and in the extension of help and hospitality to other Christians in need, even when the donors themselves are in want. In the absence of such a community, in a situation where the primacy of the fellowship of believers has given way to the church as one among many groups to which allegiance is owed, the sharing of needed resources with strangers from another congregation ceases to have any priority.

Finally, it is the compelling power of the story of God's redemption in their own lives that sets Jesus' followers apart, and grounds their sense of vocation as messengers and ministers of the good news of reconciliation through Christ. This conviction of a distinctive mission, entrusted to them by God and supported by God's comprehensive care, gives force to the New Testament's exhortations to live out a distinctive life, embodying trust in God rather than in the protection afforded by worldly power and wealth. The call to forego ordinary economic prudence in favor of reliance upon God's providence to meet basic needs is part of that larger commission. Where the idea of a distinctive vocation is gone, so is much of the rationale for the distinctive moral existence that is reflected in the New Testament's ethic of ownership.

It remains to be seen what of the canon's attitudes and norms about the treatment of wealth and possessions can still be supported within the church when these aspects of the moral world are no longer shared. What happens when the eschatological framework of the New Testament, and the centrality it claims for the story of Jesus Christ as the "hermeneutical key" to human life and identity, are no longer found credible or compelling? First, although there would obviously be no rationale for abandoning possessions for the sake of obtaining "eternal life," there might remain a kind of admiration for those who were dedicated enough to do so, even if they were finally judged "excessive" or "idealistic" (or simply misguided) in their dedication. Although the strictures against literal idolatry would be expected to remain in place, in the absence of any idea of the kingdom of God as an object of pursuit (and of the promised provision for those who pursue it), it is unlikely that any would be expected to give up possessions to ensure their loyalty to God's reign.

The norms regarding justice in the accrual and use of wealth would remain in place, although without an actual belief in the eschatological judgment of God as warrants. However, without the central focus on the story of God's grace in Christ to support the notion of all aspects of human life as gifts, the content of justice might be expected to change. The idea that humans exercise mere stewardship of the material world would be replaced by a more legalistic concept of property rights, and justice could be limited to a kind of procedural fairness; this would eliminate force and fraud, but not retain any idea that there was actual injustice in the failure to give alms when the resources existed.

The idea of God as the common Creator of humankind, and the preaching of God's universal love for God's creatures, might be expected to sustain an idea of human brother- or sisterhood (although a rather attenuated one compared to the mutual commitment expected when membership in the body of Christ is taken as the crucial constituent of identity). This could be expected to support generosity as an ideal, although there would be no foundation for real economic sacrifice and no reason for sharing to extend to an equal consideration for the needs of others. What would remain would be a positive evaluation of charitable giving and an expectation that resources over and above those needed by their owners might be given away.

In sum, in the absence of a shared and vital allegiance to the central story of Jesus Christ and the eschatological framework it presupposes, the moral force of all the aspects of the New Testament's teaching on possessions that might be labeled "extreme" would be vitiated. These include any calls to embrace poverty to secure liberty for and fidelity to God's kingdom or to make serious economic sacrifices for the sake of others' needs. They would become relics, reminders of a time when the gospel called for extraordinary loyalty, courage, and devotion. There might be a kind of nostalgia for that time, and the actions and attitudes commended in the New Testament might continue to be praised; there is no reason to expect that they would be imitated.

Thus we have found that the New Testament can offer the contemporary Christian church substantive and workable ethical guidance in the holding and use of possessions only provided that crucial conditions in the life and belief of the community are met. These conditions include engagement in a communal process of moral discernment and mutual admonition and the inhabiting of a shared "moral world" in significant continuity with the New Testament's own. I have suggested that this guidance most usefully takes the form of questions corresponding to the major themes in the New Testament's teaching regarding wealth and possessions. They are designed to highlight the reasons for which wealth and its treatment are important in the canon. These questions are not intended to replace serious engagement with particular texts and teachings, but they can help to order, clarify, and illuminate the New Testament's witness.

Selected Bibliography

Abbreviations

AB	Anchor Bible
ACNT	Augsburg Commentaries on the New Testament
Herm.	Hermeneia Commentaries
HNTC	Harper's NT Commentaries
Int.	Interpretation Commentaries
MNTC	Moffatt New Testament Commentaries
NICNT	New International Commentary on the New Testament
NIGTC	New International Greek Testament Commentaries
OTL	Old Testament Library Commentaries
SB	La Sainte Bible
TNTC	Tyndale New Testament Commentaries

Method

Birch, Bruce, and Larry Rasmussen. *Bible and Ethics in Christian Life.* Minneapolis: Augsburg Press, 1976.

Childress, James. "Scripture and Christian Ethics: Some Reflections on the Role of Scripture in Moral Deliberation and Justification," *Interpretation* 34, October 1980.

Curran, Charles. *Catholic Moral Theology in Dialogue.* South Bend: University of Notre Dame Press, 1972.

Curran, Charles, and Richard McCormick. *The Use of Scripture in Moral Theology.* New York: Paulist Press, 1984.

SELECTED BIBLIOGRAPHY

Gustafson, James. *Theology and Ethics.* Philadelphia: Pilgrim Press, 1974.

———. "The Place of Scripture in Ethics," *Interpretation* 24, October 1970.

———. "Two Approaches to Theological Ethics," *Union Seminary Quarterly Review* 26, 1968.

Hauerwas, Stanley. *A Community of Character.* Notre Dame: Notre Dame University Press, 1981.

———. *The Peaceable Kingdom.* Notre Dame: Notre Dame University Press, 1983.

Hays, Richard. "Scripture-Shaped Community: The Problem of Method in New Testament Ethics," *Interpretation* 44, January 1990.

Kelsey, David. *The Uses of Scripture in Recent Theology.* Philadelphia: Fortress Press, 1975.

Long, E. L. "The Place of the Bible in Christian Ethics," *Interpretation* 19, April 1965.

Meeks, Wayne. "The Polyphonic Ethics of the Apostle Paul," 1986 Proceedings of the Society of Christian Ethics.

Meilaender, Gilbert. *The Theory and Practice of Virtue.* Notre Dame: University of Notre Dame Press, 1984.

Miller, D. G., and D. Y. Hadidian. *Jesus and Man's Hope.* Pittsburgh: Pittsburgh Theological Seminary Press, 1971.

Niebuhr, H. Richard. *The Responsible Self.* San Francisco: Harper & Row, 1978.

Niebuhr, Reinhold. *An Interpretation of Christian Ethics.* New York: Seabury Press, 1979.

Ogletree, Thomas. *The Use of the Bible in Christian Ethics.* Philadelphia: Fortress Press, 1983.

Outka, Gene. "Character, Virtue and Narrative," *Religious Studies Review* 6/2, April 1980.

Verhey, Allen. *The Great Reversal.* Grand Rapids, MI: William B. Eerdmans Publishing Company, 1984.

Yoder, John Howard. *The Politics of Jesus.* Grand Rapids, MI: William B. Eerdmans Publishing Company, 1972.

———. "Radical Reformation Ethics," *Journal of Ecumenical Studies,* Fall 1978.

General Biblical

Aland, Kurt, Matthew Black, Carlo M. Martini, Bruce M. Metzger, and Allen Wikgren. *The Greek New Testament,* 3d ed. New York: United Bible Societies, 1975.

Bauer, Walter, William F. Arndt, F. Wilbur Gingrich, and Frederick Danker. *A Greek-English Lexicon of the New Testament and Other Early Christian Literature.* Chicago: University of Chicago Press, 1979.

Blass, F., and A. DeBrunner. *A Greek Grammar of the New Testament and Other Early Christian Literature.* Rev. by Robert W. Funk. Chicago: University of Chicago Press, 1961.

Bultmann, Rudolf. *Die Geschichte der synoptischen Tradition,* 4th ed. Goettingen, 1958.

Johnson, Luke T. *The Writings of the New Testament: An Interpretation.* Philadelphia: Fortress Press, 1986.

Kuemmel, W. *An Introduction to the New Testament.* Nashville: Abingdon Press, 1975.

Metzger, Bruce. *A Textual Commentary on the Greek New Testament,* 3d ed. New York: United Bible Societies, 1971.

Moule, C. F. D. *An Idiom Book of the Greek New Testament.* New York: Cambridge University Press, 1959.

Schmidt, Thomas. *Hostility to Wealth in the Synoptic Gospels.* Sheffield: JSOT Press, 1987.

Zerwick, Max, and Mary Grosvener. *A Grammatical Analysis of the New Testament,* volume I. Rome: Biblical Institute Press, 1974.

Mark

Best, Ernest. *Disciples and Discipleship: Studies in the Gospel According to Mark.* Edinburgh: T & T Clark, 1986.

Hengel, Martin. *Studies in the Gospel of Mark.* London: SCM, 1985.

Kee, Howard. *Community of the New Age: Studies in Mark's Gospel.* Philadelphia: Westminster Press, 1977.

Kelber, Werner. *The Kingdom in Mark: A New Time and Place.* Philadelphia: Fortress Press, 1974.

Lane, William. *The Gospel According to Mark.* Grand Rapids, MI: William B. Eerdmans Publishing Company, 1974.

Marxsen, Willi. *Mark the Evangelist: Studies on the Redaction-History of the Gospel.* Nashville: Abingdon Press, 1969.

Myers, Ched. *Binding the Strong Man: A Political Reading of Mark's Story of Jesus.* Maryknoll, NY: Orbis Books, 1985.

Senior, Donald. "With Swords and Clubs: The Setting of Mark's Community," *Biblical Theology Bulletin* 17, 1987.

Tolbert, M. A. *Sowing the Gospel: Mark's World in Literary-Historical Perspective.* Minneapolis: Fortress Press, 1989.

Via, Dan O. *The Ethics of Mark's Gospel — In the Middle of Time.* Philadelphia: Fortress Press, 1985.

Luke

Danker, Frederick. *Benefactor: Epigraphic Study of a Greco-Roman and New Testament Semantic Field.* St. Louis: Clayton Publishing House, 1982.

Downing, F. G. *Christ and the Cynics.* Sheffield: Sheffield Academic Press, 1988.

Eaton, B. S. *The Purpose of Acts.* London: S.P.C.K., 1936.

Ellis, E. E. *The Gospel of Luke.* Grand Rapids, MI: William B. Eerdmans Publishing Company, 1974.

Fitzmyer, J. A. (AB) *The Gospel According to Luke I–IX.* New York: Doubleday, 1983.

Johnson, Luke T. *The Literary Function of Possessions in Luke-Acts.* Missoula: Scholars Press, 1977.

———. *Sharing Possessions.* Philadelphia: Fortress Press, 1981.

———. *The Gospel of Luke.* Collegeville, MN: Liturgical Press, 1991.

Mack, B. *A Myth of Innocence.* Philadelphia: Fortress Press, 1988.

Marshall, I. Howard. (NIGTC) *The Gospel of Luke.* Grand Rapids, MI: William B. Eerdmans Publishing Company, 1978.

Moessner, D. *Lord of the Banquet: Literary and Theological Significance of Luke's Travel Narrative.* Philadelphia: Fortress Press, 1989.

Seccombe, David. *Possessions and the Poor in Luke-Acts.* Linz: Studien zum Neuen Testament und seiner Umwelt, 1982.

Talbert, C. *Reading Luke.* New York: Crossroad, 1982.

Tannehill, Robert. *The Narrative Unity of Luke-Acts.* New York: Fortress Press, 1986.

II Corinthians

Barnett, A. *Paul Becomes a Literary Influence.* Chicago: University of Chicago Press, 1941.
Baur, F. C. *Paulus der Apostel Jesu Christi,* 2nd ed. Leipzig: L. W. Reisland, 1866.
Best, Ernest. (Int.) *II Corinthians.* Atlanta: John Knox Press, 1987.
Betz, Hans Dieter. (Herm.) *2 Corinthians 8 and 9.* Philadelphia: Fortress Press, 1985.
Bultmann, Rudolf. *The Second Letter to the Corinthians.* Minneapolis: Augsburg Publishing House, 1985.
Dahl, Nils. *Studies in Paul.* Minneapolis: Augsburg Publishing House, 1977.
Danker, Frederick. *Benefactor: Epigraphic Study of a Greco-Roman and New Testament Semantic Field.* St. Louis: Clayton Publishing House, 1982.
———. (ACNT) *II Corinthians.* Minneapolis: Augsburg Publishing House, 1989.
Furnish, V. P. (AB) *II Corinthians.* New York: Doubleday, 1984.
Georgi, D. *Die Geschichte der Kollekte der Paulus fuer Jerusalem.* Hamburg: Reich, 1965.
Munck, J. *Paul and the Salvation of Mankind.* English ed. tr. F. Clarke. Richmond: Knox Press, 1959.
Stephenson, A. *The Authorship and Integrity of the New Testament.* London: S.P.C.K., 1965.
Windisch, W. *Der Zweite Korintherbrief.* Goettingen: Vandenhoeck and Ruprecht, 1924.
Young, Frances, and David Ford. *Meaning and Truth in II Corinthians.* Cambridge: Cambridge University Press, 1987.

James

Adamson, J. B. *James: The Man and His Message.* Grand Rapids, MI: William B. Eerdmans Publishing Company, 1989.

———. (NICNT) *James.* Grand Rapids, MI: William B. Eerdmans Publishing Company, 1976.

Cantinat, J. (SB) *Les Epitres de S. Jacques et de S. Jude.* Paris, 1973.

Davids, Peter. (NIGTC) *The Epistle of James.* Grand Rapids, MI: William B. Eerdmans Publishing Company, 1982.

Dibelius, M. *Der Brief der Jakobus,* Goettingen: Vandenhoeck and Ruprecht, 1920. English ed. tr. H. Greeven. *James.* Philadelphia: Fortress Press, 1976.

Johnson, Luke T. "The Use of Leviticus 19 in the Epistle of James," *Journal of Biblical Literature* 101, 1982.

Kennedy, H. A. "The Hellenistic Atmosphere of the Epistle of James," *Expositor,* volume 2, 1911.

Laws, S. (HNTC) *A Commentary on the Epistle of St James.* New York: Harper & Row, 1980.

Massebreau, L. "L'epitre de Jacque — est-elle l'oeuvre d'un Cretien?" *Revue de l'Histoire des Religions* 32, 1895.

Maynard-Reid, P. *Poverty and Wealth in James.* Maryknoll, NY: Orbis Books, 1987.

Moffat, J. (MNTC) *The General Epistles.* London: Hodder & Stoughton, 1948.

Moo, Douglas. (TNTC) *James.* Grand Rapids, MI: William B. Eerdmans Publishing Company, 1985.

Mussner, Franz. *Der Jakobsbrief.* Herders Theologische Kommentar zur Neuen Testament. Freiburg, 1967.

Schrage, W. "Der Jakobsbrief," *Die Katholischen Briefen* NTD 10, Goettingen, 1973.

Spitta, F. "Der Brief der Jakobus," *Zur Geschichte und Litteratur des Urchristentums.* Goettingen, 1896.

Index of Proper Names